MOVIE FANTASTIC

Beyond the Dream Machine

KING KONG

MOVIE FANTASTIC
Beyond the Dream Machine

David Annan

Bounty Books

Designed by Peter Warne Associates

Library of Congress Catalog Card Number: 74-81687

This Edition is published by Bounty Books
a division of Crown Publishers Inc.
by arrangement with Lorrimer Publishing Limited

ISBN 0-517-518139

Made and printed in Great Britain by
Lowe & Brydone (Printers) Ltd., Thetford, Norfolk

CONTENTS

ACKNOWLEDGEMENTS

The publishers wish to thank the following organizations for their help in preparing this book: the British Film Institute, 20th Century Fox, MGM-EMI, Columbia-Warner, United Artists, Allied Artists, Paramount, Disney, Universal MCA, RKO Pictures, Rank, First National, Cinema International Corporation, Hammer, the Cinema Bookshop, the Munich Stadtmuseum and the Frankfurt Goethe Museum.

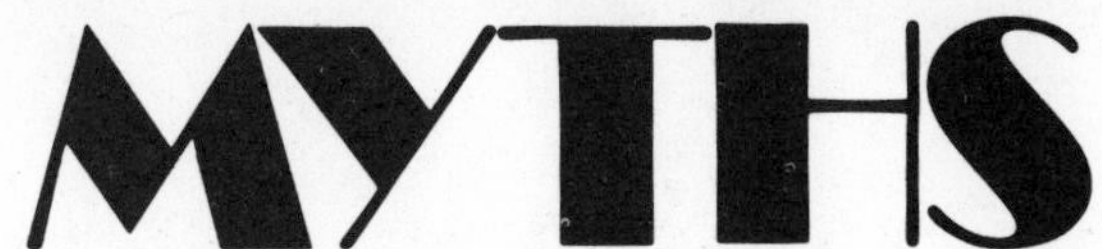

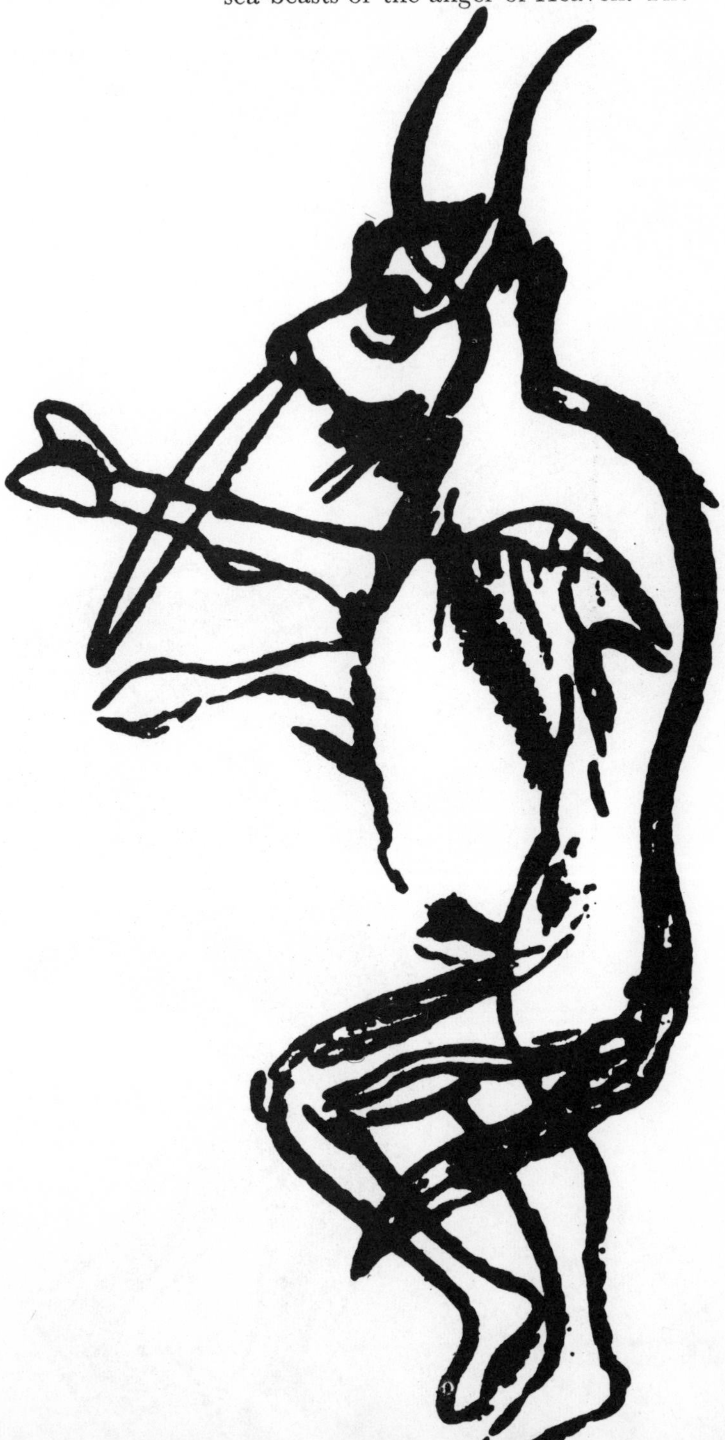

Monsters from space are as old as the gods and myths of men. Primitive tribes living in caves saw the thunder and the lightning as the work of sky giants, while floods were the fault of huge sea-beasts or the anger of Heaven. The

natural disasters which afflicted men were given monstrous or unearthly causes. Catastrophes of the past were remembered in songs and epics. Fears of future destruction were lumped into the person of demons and divinities, who were then worshipped to allay their wrath. The belief in the supernatural and the need for rituals or shows to appease gods and devils are more ancient than our recorded history.

Pictorial art began as an act of worship and commemoration. The caves at Trois-Frères, where the earliest European art begins, show hunters at the chase of beasts, also witch-doctors. The human and the animal combine in magic. The drawings are the forerunners of the Cretan Minotaur, or the half-human, half-beasts from the book by H. G. Wells, *The Island of Doctor Moreau.*

Primitive drawings from the caves of the Trois-Frères, France (also on preceding page).

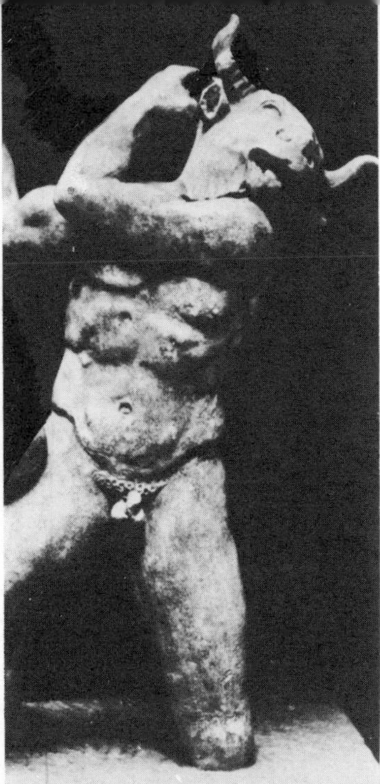

Classical statue of the Minotaur, the half-bull and half-man in the centre of the Cretan labyrinth.

Dr. Moreau's humanoid creations, from the film version of H. G. Wells' book, called *Island of Lost Souls* (1932).

The painter was both remembering his skill and ensuring in pictures that his food supply would continue. In much of primitive art, particularly in the masks of dancers, men-beasts are a favourite theme. The wolf-man of the Hopi Indian dance is religious, while the werewolves of medieval European legend were demoniacal, although they ended in horror films as straight bogey figures.

The earliest recorded epic, Gilgamesh, which is some 4,000 years old, deals with a tragic Assyrian hero who fights monsters and visits the dead and embodies many of the themes of the supernatural that still haunt the cinema. Gilgamesh is both god and man; his companion is Enkidu, a wild man reared by animals. They vanquish the giant Humbaba, who lives in a magic forest and is Evil; they also kill the

A Katchina totem doll in the form of a wolf-dancer, made by the Hopi Indians.

The monster from *I Was a Teenage Werewolf* (1957).

raging Bull of Heaven. Enkidu dies, and Gilgamesh wanders after his soul through the wilderness and into the mountain above the Underworld and the sea of the dead. His journey is as unearthly and valiant as Douglas Fairbanks' journey in *The Thief of Bagdad*; in this, the hero also enters a mountain, flies through the air, passes through a magic forest of man-trees, crosses the sea of the Underworld, and plunges below it to retrieve the secret of life. Gilgamesh is the first recorded hero who travels through time and space and death, and his cosmic encounters have inspired magic images to this day.

Without believing the occult writers and British Israelites who claim that the Pharoahs knew all the secrets of

Douglas Fairbanks Snr. flies away on his magic carpet over his victorious army in *The Thief of Bagdad* (1924).

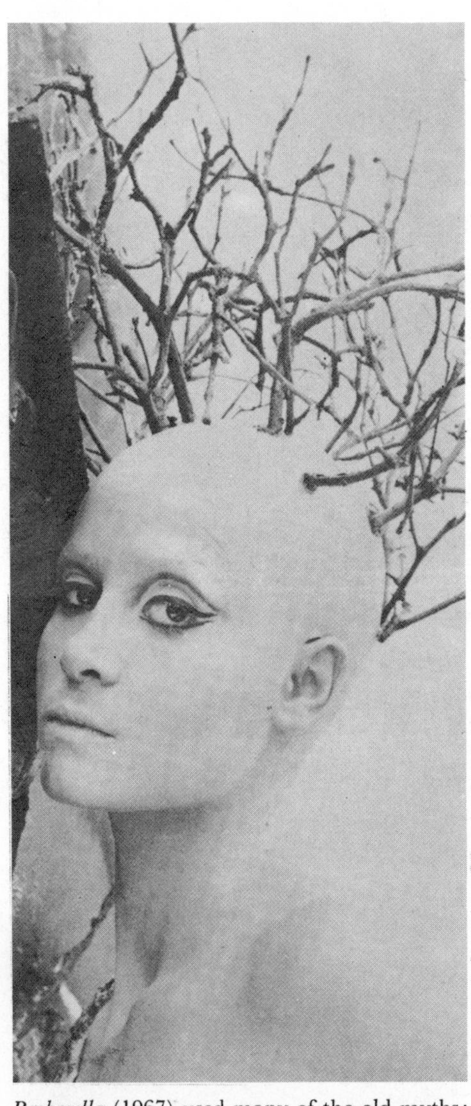

Barbarella (1967) used many of the old myths: here, Fabienne Fabre plays the tree-woman.

Women are rocks and trees in this hellish fantasy on Dante's *Inferno*, from *Barbarella*.

The falcon-headed god Ament, with his flying serpent disc above him, taken from an Ancient Egyptian tomb painting.

A mummified princess, a severed hand on her belly, lies ready for reincarnation in *Blood from the Mummy's Tomb* (1971).

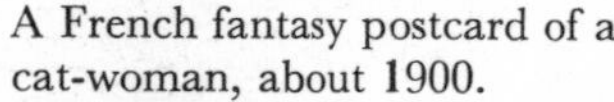

A French fantasy postcard of a cat-woman, about 1900.

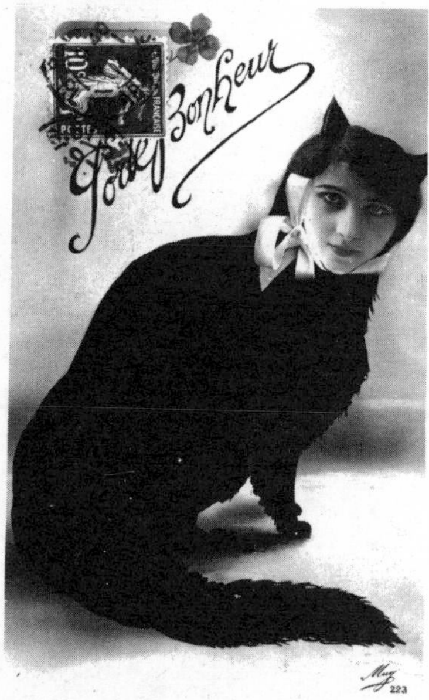

Simone Simon in *Cat-People* (1942), produced by Val Lewton and directed by Jacques Tourneur.

The black cat in Makavejev's *The Switchboard Operator* (1967) represents both sex and the future death of the girl.

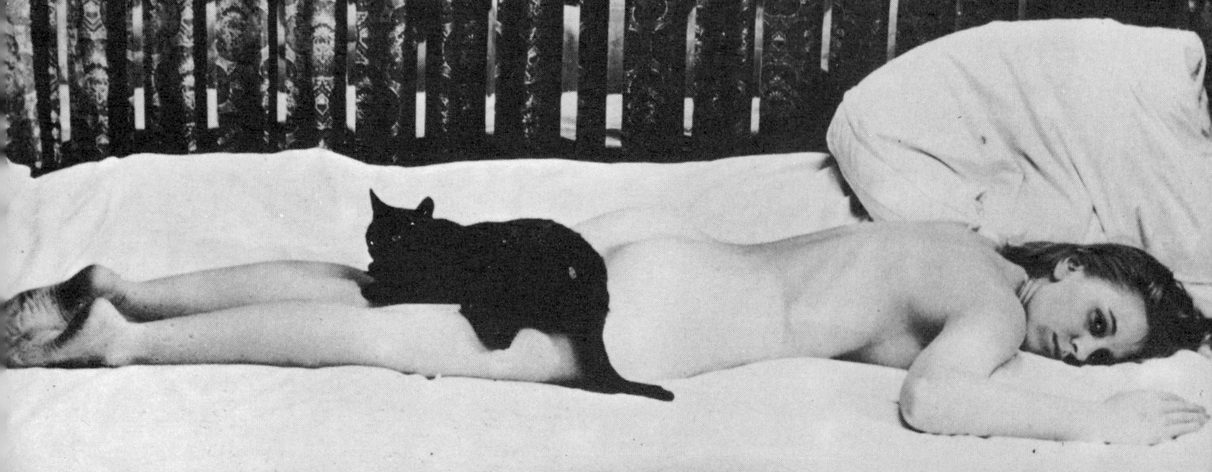

mechanics and telekinesis and space-travel, the winged gods of ancient Egypt, such as Horus and Ament, who flew as a falcon or a feathered disc, are basic to the mythology behind much of science fiction. From the mathematical mysteries of the Great Pyramid to the symbolism of the beast-gods, many Egyptian preoccupations with life and death have become staples of the supernatural. The whole cycle of Balkan films about tombs and revived corpses originally springs from Egypt and the cult of the dead and the Mummy. The terrors of Transylvania and Dracula lie much later in history. French fantasies about cat-women and Val Lewton's minor classic, *The Cat People*, owe less to Middle Europe than to the Middle East, from where sprang the original fear of death in the form of a black cat.

The mythology of the Greeks and Romans contributed little to the fantasy side of making pictures outside Harryhausen's fine work in his *Jason and the Argonauts*, and the title of *Dr Cyclops*, the Schoedsack movie where the mad Doctor, played by Albert Dekker, shrinks Janice Logan and her friends smaller than Ulysses seemed to the original Homeric monster. The Italian cycle of Hercules films have some giant and monster effects, but their chief merit was to prove Joe Levine right – publicity can sell anything. *Hercules Unchained* was the foundation of Levine's film fortune; but it was the victory of promotion over production value. More enduring to later science fiction films was the mechanical tradition of the classical civilisations. Both Archimedes and Vergil were meant to have built robot men, Archimedes to defend the walls of Syracuse, while Vergil's bronze archers were guards on his own house. Ovid's *Metamorphoses* tapped a rich vein of mutation between man and animal, which was to be a recurring theme of the fantasy cinema.

Neptune lends a hand in *Jason and the Argonauts* (1963).

Janice Logan under the boot of *Dr. Cyclops* (1940).
The shrunken humans retaliate in *Dr. Cyclops*.

Steve Reeves as Hercules shows off his strength in *Hercules Unchained* (1958).

The creation of the mechanised Maria in Fritz Lang's *Metropolis* (1926).

The bronze giant menaces the Greeks in *Jason and the Argonauts* (1963).

By their concentration on astronomy and mathematics and rationalism, the Greeks introduced the theme of mechanistic gods and a controllable universe. They diminished the value of their legendary gods and of a world of terrors and magic. The particular god who flourished in the new thinking was the lame Hephaestus, the god of metallurgy and invention, whom the Romans called Vulcan. In his most famous legend, he constructed a bronze net more invisible than a cobweb and hung it over his marriage-bed to entrap his wife, the Goddess of Love, with her lover, the God of War. He was also reputed to have a set of golden mechanical women to help him in his smithy, thus becoming the direct forerunner of Rotwang in *Metropolis*, who constructed an assistant robot and the mechanical Maria to confuse the workers of the underground city. Perhaps Hephaestus' most famous creation was the bronze giant Talos who could only be destroyed when a pin was removed from his ankle and the ichor ran out of his veins. This legend began centuries of variation on the theme of a mechanical monster with one fatal flaw, a metal Achilles only vulnerable through its heel or another secret weakness.

The Greeks also introduced the most powerful theme of films of fantasy – the concept of a man driven by his lust for knowledge to his own final destruction. In the legend, Prometheus stole from the gods the useful arts such as architecture and metalworking and medicine, and he passed them on to mankind, which he even created in some versions of the myth. Above all, he stole the terrible gift of fire. As a punishment for revealing the secret of warmth and devastation, he was chained on a rock with his liver devoured by a vulture for all time. The thirst for knowledge and experiment is insatiable and leads to the destruction of the inventor. So, too,

Icarus ignored the advice of his father Daedalus and flew too near the sun on his man-made wings, which melted and plunged the youth to his death. Icarus and Prometheus are the true forerunners of Count Frankenstein, the rational scientist pursuing his researches to his own end. In fact, Mary Shelley, who wrote the original novel of Frankenstein, subtitled it *The Modern Prometheus*.

Count Frankenstein is horrified with the monster he has created. This drawing is taken from the original frontispiece to Mary Shelley's novel *Frankenstein*.

Prometheus creating mankind, from an ancient Greek frieze.

Boris Karloff, playing Count Frankenstein's monster, is tortured by fire in James Whale's original version of *Frankenstein* (1931).

A drawing taken from a relief in an ancient tomb at Palenque, Mexico.

Thus the Greeks introduced the theme of science into films of fantasy – the idea of a mechanical monster, controlled by reason, made by invention. This was the reverse side of the ancient myths of natural or divine monsters, created by storm or vasty deep, infernal and horrible. After the Greeks, the theme of robots counterbalanced the theme of super-beasts. According to some writers, other civilisations such as the Mayans may also have invented robot gods. Certainly the relief of the so-called spaceman at Palenque does prophesy *2001.* And while the legend of the winged messiah Quetzalcoatl may not be an actual description of an ancient space-traveller, the helmeted statues of Veracruz and Easter Island look dressed for the first voyage to the moon. Some Mayan boys were seen recently leaving their village in Yucatan to perform the

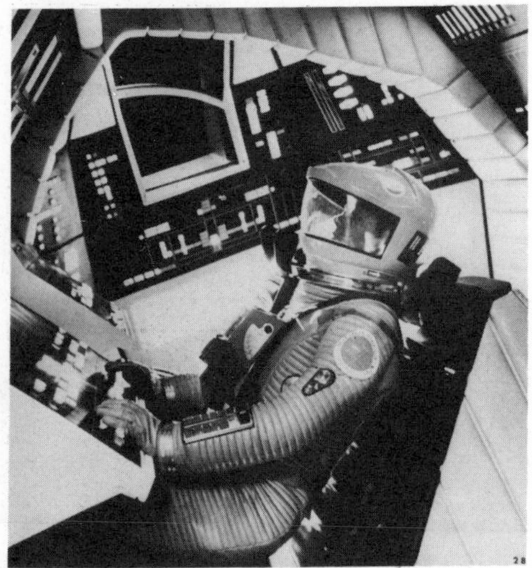

An astronaut in Stanley Kubrick's *2001* (1968).

A stone head from Veracruz, Mexico.

A Mayan tribal chieftain wearing a headress symbolising the winged god Quetzalcoatl, taken from a pot excavated at Tikal, Guatemala.

An altar scene from *Eyes of Hell* (1961

ancient dance of the bird-god against the hunter. They had dropped their traditional feathered costumes to wear Batman cloaks and masks. To them, Batman was the fourth reincarnation of Quetzalcoatl to come to Mayan Mexico since Cortes. Mythology lives on in modern serials.

Because Mexico is, indeed, the nearest country with an ancient civilisation close to Hollywood, the art of the pre-Columbians has much influenced the look of fantasy films. It may be rare to find the most famous of the jade Mayan death-masks actually reproduced. But the foetal look of the early civilisations of Veracruz and the jaguar-gods of the Olmecs have come back to haunt our science-fiction. The art of old civilisations often embodies the archetypes of mankind now reproduced for mass fantasies.

A mask from Veracruz, Mexico.

An Olmec stone jaguar-god.

The Man from Planet X (1951).

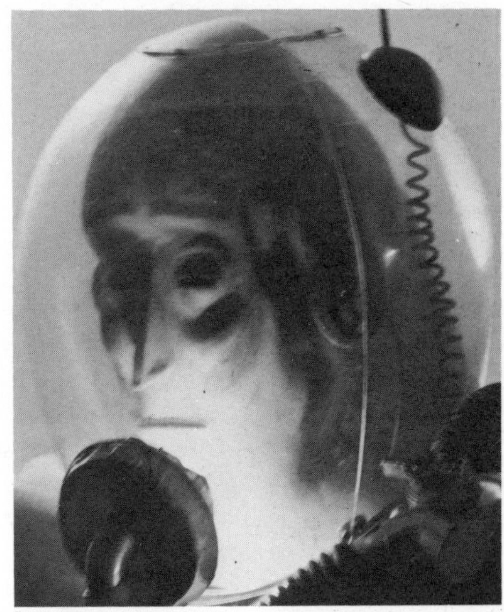

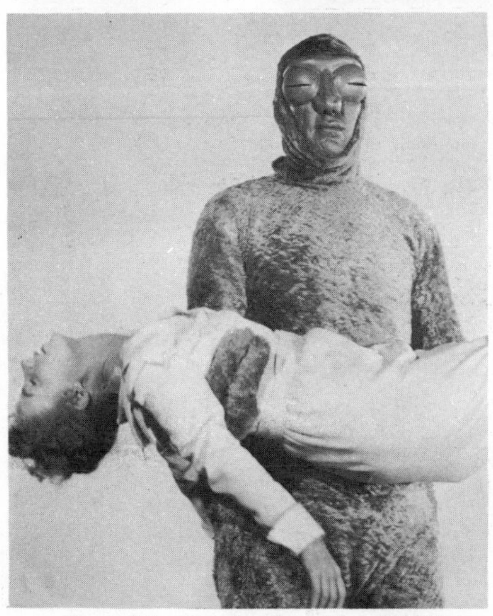

One of the *Invaders from Mars* (1959).

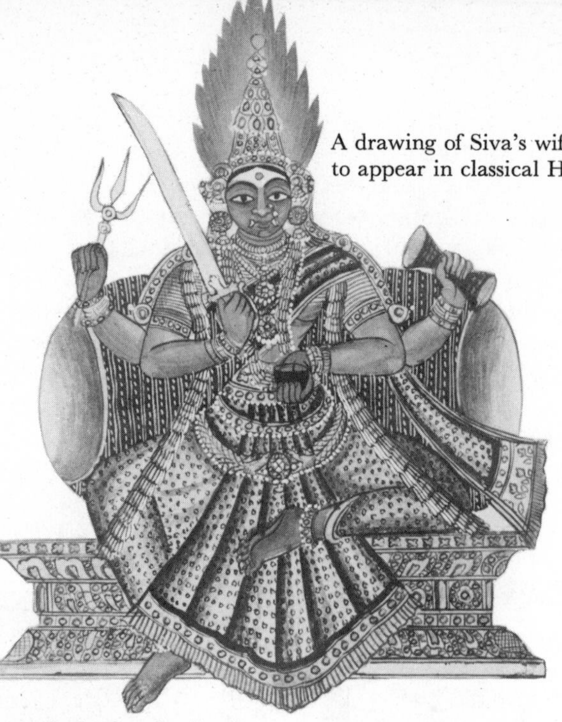

A drawing of Siva's wife as she was supposed to appear in classical Hindu mythology.

Other ancient mythologies in India and China and Japan have spawned the supernatural films of today. Magic is a staple part of the endless serials churned out in Bombay and Hong Kong. The actors dressed as gods leap in one shot and land five miles away in the next one. In a recent Taiwanese serial shown weekly in San Francisco's Chinatown, the same five warrior girls ride a magic bird, blind their enemies with leaves thrown through the air, fight giant beasts, and rely on the protection of Shamans with electric particles of force radiating from the platters on their hands. Hindu and Chinese mythology has had a profound effect on present taste in popular Eastern movies – Siva's wife, for instance, has fangs and a bowl for blood. In a more serious vein, a Japanese film such as *Kwaidan* relies heavily on the legends of ghosts that still occupy a major place in traditional thought. Only the sword of the strongest Samurai is metal and sharp enough to rout the monsters of legend and fear.

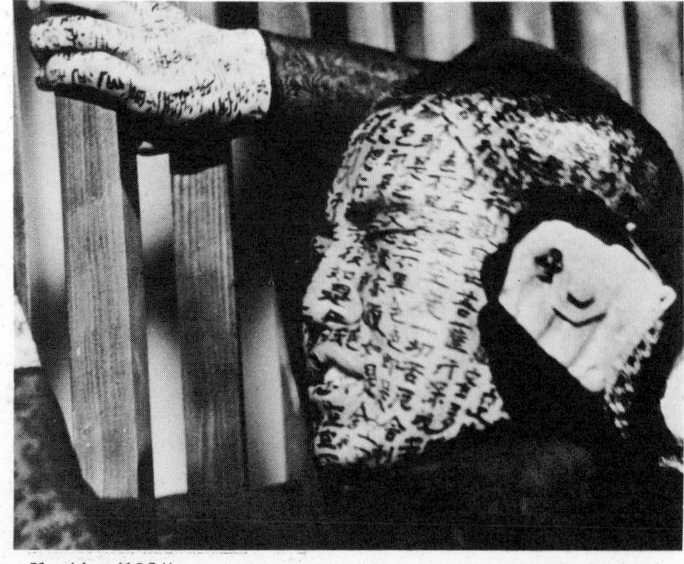

The ghosts from *Kwaidan* (1964).

In the dark ages of Europe after the fall of Rome, Christianity preached a religion of love in contradiction to the primitive cults of the barbarian tribes. Like other religions, Christianity did not replace, but overlaid more savage faiths. The holy terrors of Celtic beliefs were turned into the beasts of Revelation and the demons inside the Gaderene swine. An old monster poem such as Beowulf was given a Christian veneer of repentance and redemption. In medieval cathedrals, the fear of devils was built into the structure, with gargoyles under the choir stalls and on the gutters. The monsters on the roof of Notre Dame are the stone ancestors and mockers of Charles Laughton's own twisted form as the Hunchback. Also on the roof of Notre Dame are the statues of the Seven Deadly Sins which Karloff melts with his Radium-X touch after each revenge murder in *The Invisible Ray*. The same sins led to the death of the critics at the hands of Vincent Price in *Theatre of Blood*, while the actual apparatus of torture used by the medieval Church to torment heretics and drive out devils, gave the mechanics of horror to later times. Hell and the Inquisition were the evil laboratory of the soul.

Charles Laughton watches the Paris mob from the cathedral door in *The Hunchback of Notre Dame* (1939).

The tortures of Hell in a medieval drawing of 1496.

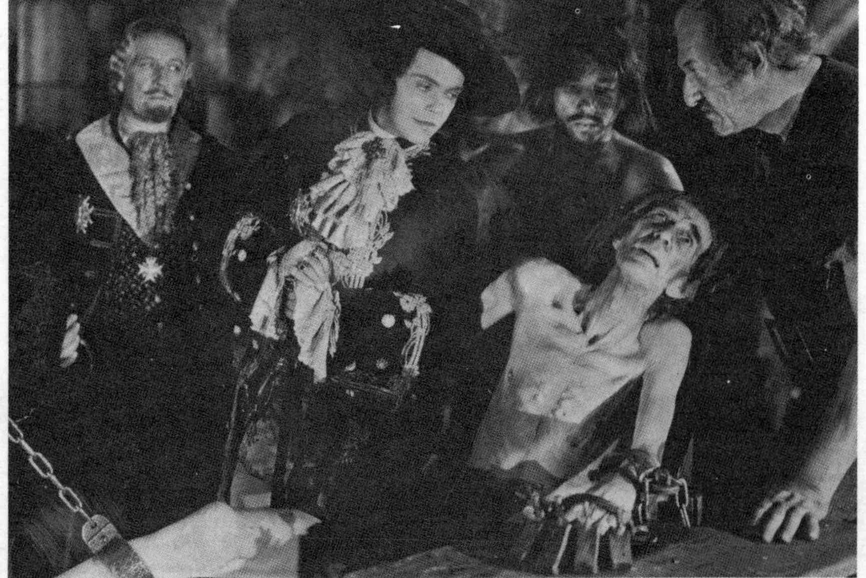

A torture sequence by weight and chain from James Whale's *The Man in the Iron Mask* (1939).

A myth that influenced the Chinese, the Hindus and particularly the Egyptians was the myth of the egg that created life. Not only was the egg the universal creator, but also the shape of the world. This belief later influenced the alchemists, who saw in the egg the shape of the philosopher's stone which would transmute base metals into gold and make the dead alive again. It is interesting that the monsters of science fiction sometimes revert to the shape of the egg. When The Thing comes out of the sea in the Japanese epic to meet Godzilla, it is in the shape of a gigantic egg. So is the basic shape of the monster on *The Angry Red Planet.* The symbols of our dreams recur in the fantasy films of today.

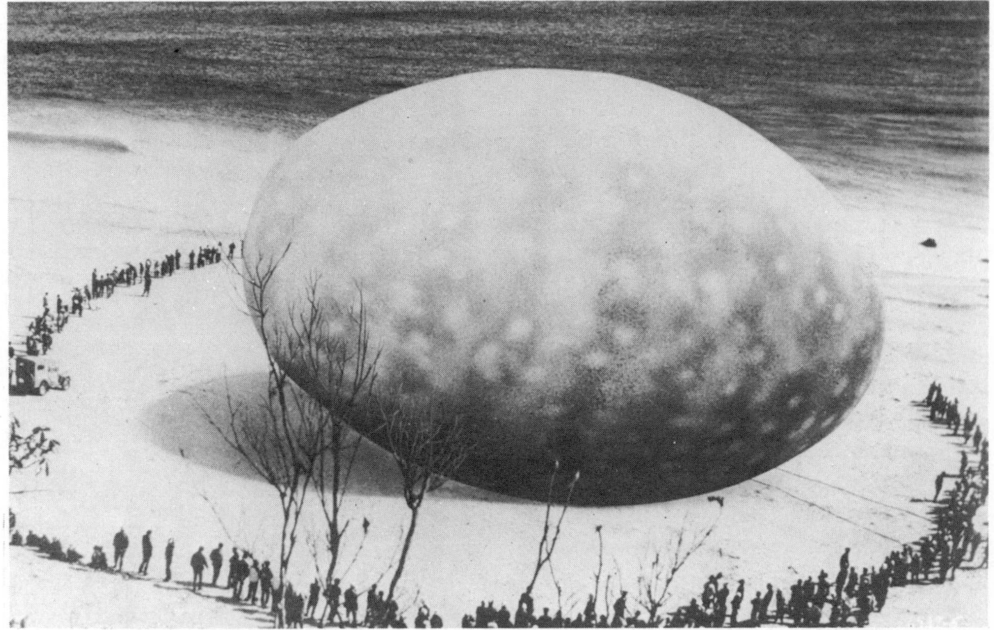

A crowd watches the birth of the monster in *Godzilla versus The Thing* (1964).

The monster approaches in *The Angry Red Planet* (1960).

The Four Horsemen of the Apocalypse, from the Cologne Bible of 1479.

In these scenes from Ingmar Bergman's *Seventh Seal* (1956), the Penitents whip themselves into a frenzy, the Knight plays chess with Death, and the main characters finally dance away to die.

Death was a familiar figure in the Middle Ages. He was not an abstraction. He was a being who knocked on the door and carried away his victims. His outriders were the other three Horsemen of the Apocalyse, Famine, Plague, and War. The images of these terrible horsemen rode the films of Murnau and Stroheim and even one of Valentino's, but it was Bergman's *The Seventh Seal* which best captured the person of Death and the fear of the plague. The Knight struggles with Death by playing a game of chess with him; by cheating, he allows the clown and his wife and child to escape again the Massacre of the Innocents. There is a self-deceiving Witch who believes she is possessed, and is not; an evil and cruel Doctor; a fierce mocker of a monk with a face like Savanarola; and the Knight himself whose "whole life has been a meaningless search" and now must die in the Dance of Death. It is a film of terrible power and evocation of past obsessions.

Of the many images of the Middle Ages, the living skeleton is the most haunting. Often depicted were mythological orchestras of the dead, which danced above the plague pits. In our times, even Walt Disney once, in his early days, animated a dance of skeletons on Halloween Night. But the great Harryhausen again was the one who brought to life the dangerous skeletons from the legend of the Dragon's Teeth, which sprang up as warriors when sown on the ground. Skeletons remained a favourite shock device even in space fiction. And they hung in the closets of the alchemists, who were bred by the Middle Ages to be the first mad scientists of our traditions.

Todd Armstrong as Jason fights his skeleton enemies.

The skeletons' ball from a woodcut of 1493.

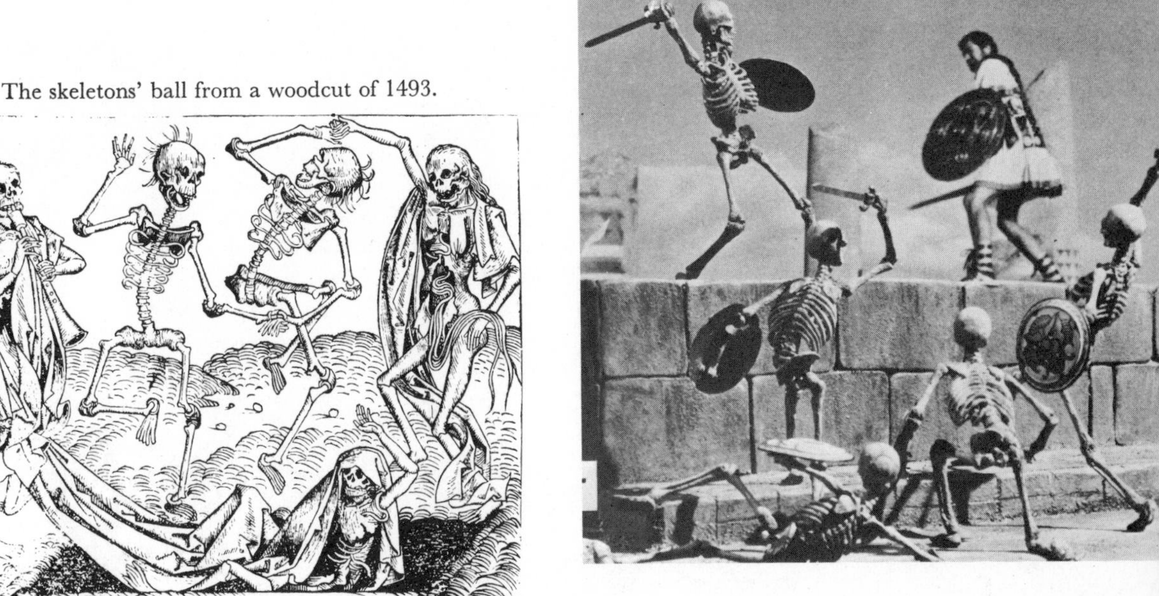

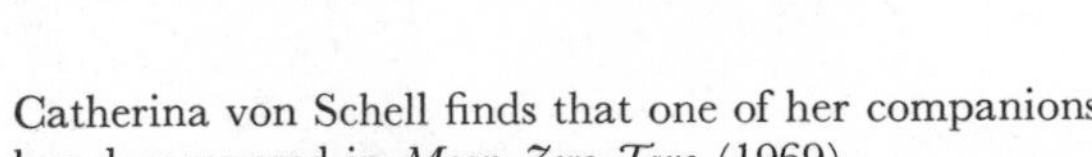

Catherina von Schell finds that one of her companions has decomposed in *Moon Zero Two* (1969).

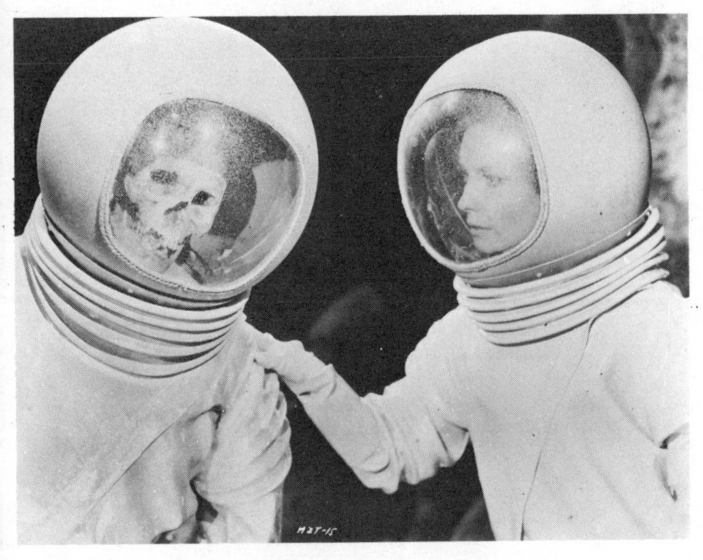

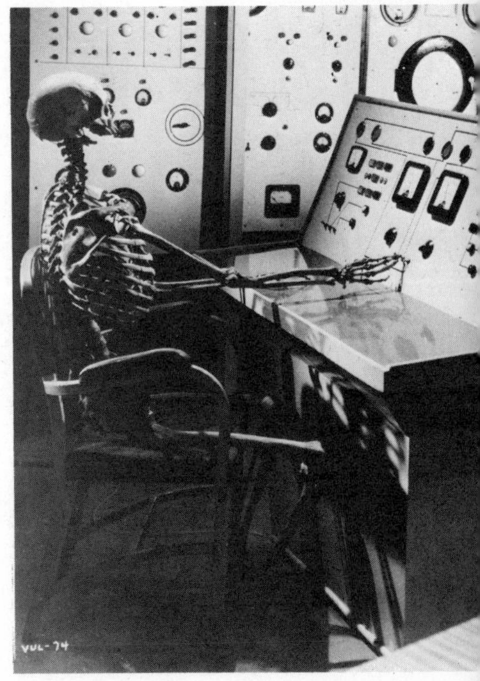

A skeleton sits at a console table in *The Vulture* (1966).

The alchemists were the bridge between mythology and science. The greatest of them all, Paracelsus, used traditional medicines such as viper's fat and unicorn's horn and mummy powder to make his patients more ill, but he also put the new Renaissance practice of experiment into operation. He did not want to dissect dead bodies to learn the secret of life, but living ones. Not for him the bodysnatching of the anatomists, but researches into amputation and transplant. He rebelled against the legend of Doctor Faustus that made the pursuit of knowledge part of a pact with the Devil. For Paracelsus, "the scientist conquers Hell." He returned to the Greek tradition of the inventor mastering nature, not conjuring up the demons of fear and the subconscious. While other necromancers went out to churchyards to raise the dead, Paracelsus tried to solve the problems of the human body and the universe. He stood halfway between the laboratory and the Kabbala, like the great Rabbi Loew of Prague who created the monster Golem

An early dissection, taken from a medieval woodcut.

An early amputation, from a sixteenth-century woodcut.

Two Elizabethan alchemists, John Dee and Edmund Kelly, raising the dead, from Dee's memoirs, published in 1659.

from magic books to save his people.

The legend of the Golem is, indeed, both a catalyst of past tradition and a root cause of our fantasies. The Golem fed on the folk idea of the monster which rises to save its people, then turns to ravage them. Although the Golem is man-made, it is created in the way that the gods of Mesopotamia made men, by breathing life into wet clay. It does not work by a machine, but by a Star of Judah in its breast, by faith alone. The Golem inspired Mary Shelley's concept of Frankenstein as a neutral monster, able to do good and evil depending on its treatment by men. It also was the subject of the first masterpiece of the monster in the German cinema, and thus the direct source of all other monster films. Paul Wegener's direction and portrayal of the second version of *The Golem* in 1920 displayed styles of lighting (taken from Reinhardt) and design and techniques of controlled acting that have influenced Karloff and his imitators to this day.

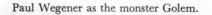

Paul Wegener as the monster Golem.

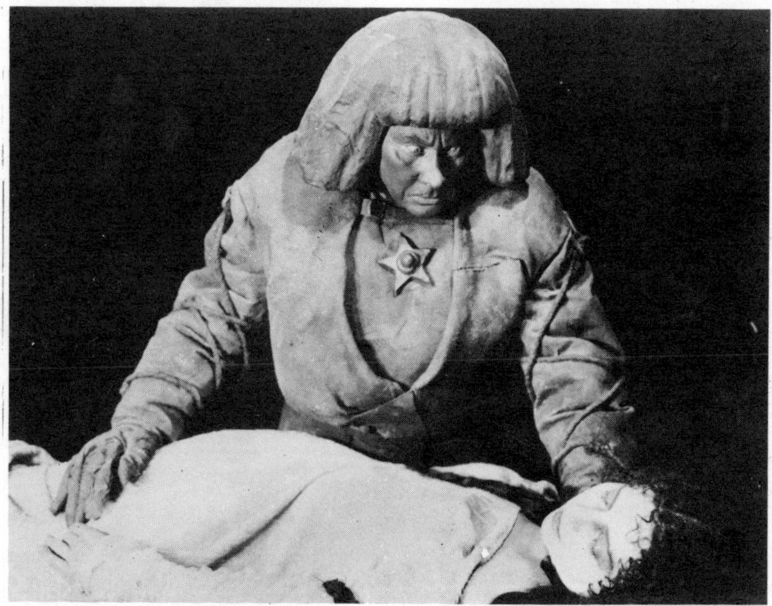

King Dracula Vlad enjoys a meal, while watching his victims being chopped into small pieces and impaled, from a woodcut of 1500.

Against the legends of Doctor Faustus and Rabbi Loew, who pursued knowledge for its power, there is a darker tradition in Central Europe, that of the Rumanian King Dracula, Vlad the Impaler, and of the Hungarian Countess, Elizabeth Bathory. These two bloodthirsty historical figures are the breeders of the legends of Dracula and the vampires from Transylvania. While Dracula Vlad drove stakes through thousands of living victims to kill them in agony, legend made a wooden stake the only end for the undead vampire in his coffin. As for the Countess Bathory, she used the blood of her girl victims for her baths, seeking eternal youth. It is no coincidence that the first masterpiece about vampires, Murnau's *Nosferatu*, was made a year before *The Golem*, nor that little more than a hundred years before on Lake Geneva, Lord Byron should have inspired his companion Polidori to write down the first novel called *The Vampire* at the same time as Mary Shelley wrote her *Frankenstein*. The tradition of the human bloodsucker and of the undead is always the rival of the tradition of the man-made monster created by the lust for knowledge.

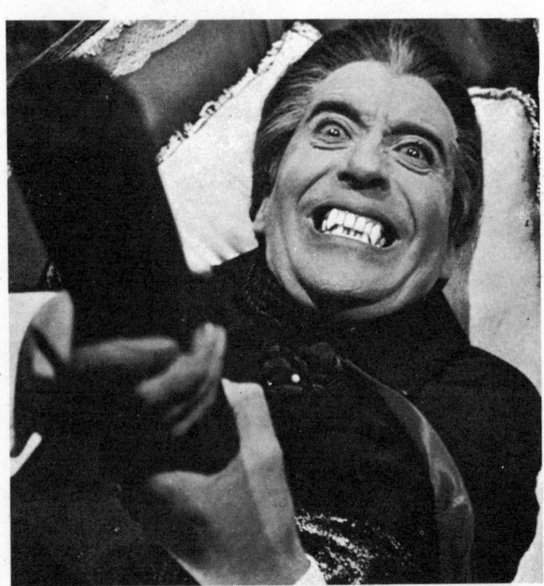

Christopher Lee attempts to pull the stake from his chest in *Dracula has Risen from the Grave* (1968).

Max Schreck as the original screen Dracula in *Nosferatu* (1922), looking for more victims.

Another classical and medieval tradition that was a staple of the fantasy film was the idea of the maiden as victim. Girls were sacrificed to the bull-headed Minotaur in Crete, Andromeda was bound on her rock to satisfy the sea-beast. This situation became the favourite cliché of the monster movie, with the great freak threatening the screaming maiden in white just before the arrival of a modern Perseus to save her from her fate. In the Middle Ages, the sacrificial virgin was set out as a trap as much as a victim. By tradition, the fabulous unicorn could only be caught by laying his head in a maiden's lap. This overt sexual allegory also became part of the horror film, in which the horn became the knife that threatened the girl, laid out for the sacrifice by devil worshippers or set up for sexual sadists with the lust of Jack the Ripper. It could also become the tentacle of the monster entrapping the victim.

Raquel Welch in the claws of a prehistoric bird in *One Million Years B.C.* (1966). The special effects were again by Ray Harryhausen.

Charles Gray prepares his victim for the sacrificial knife in *The Devil Rides Out* (1968).

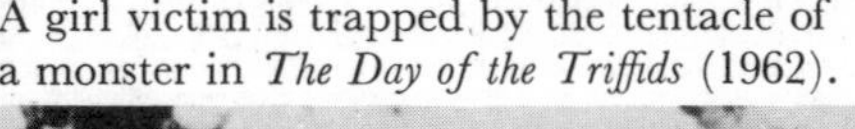

A girl victim is trapped by the tentacle of a monster in *The Day of the Triffids* (1962).

Even with the growing spirit of scientific enquiry that came out of the Renaissance and the Reformation, the violent fantasies that grew out of the religious wars between Catholics and Protestants resulted in a revival of the persecution of heretics and witches, and the search for demons and devils. What vision of Edgar Allen Poe's or Roger Corman's can equal the reality of the Iron Maiden, used for the examination of traitors? The persecution of witches in *The Witchfinder-General* was based on the real career of those Puritan per-

The Iron Maiden, a torture instrument with internal spikes, invented in the 16th century.

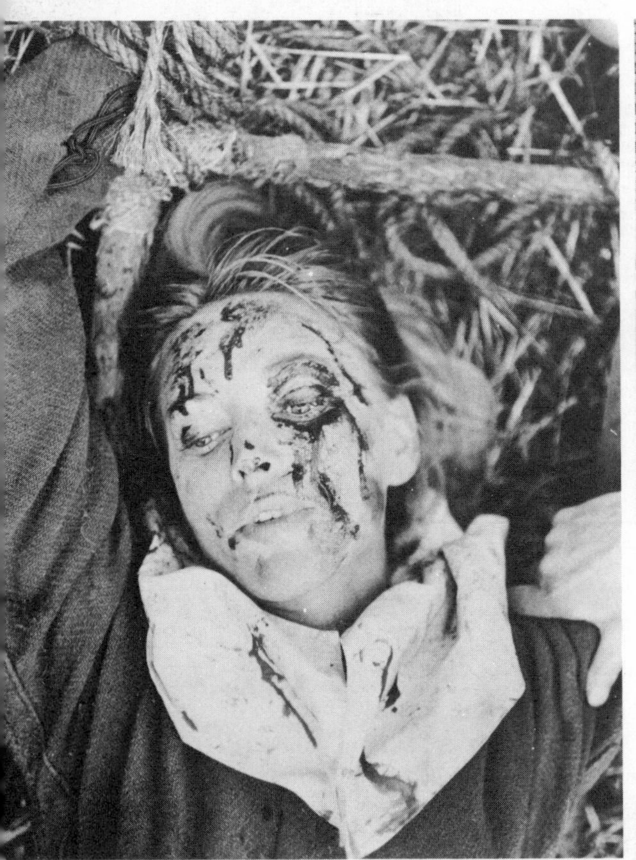

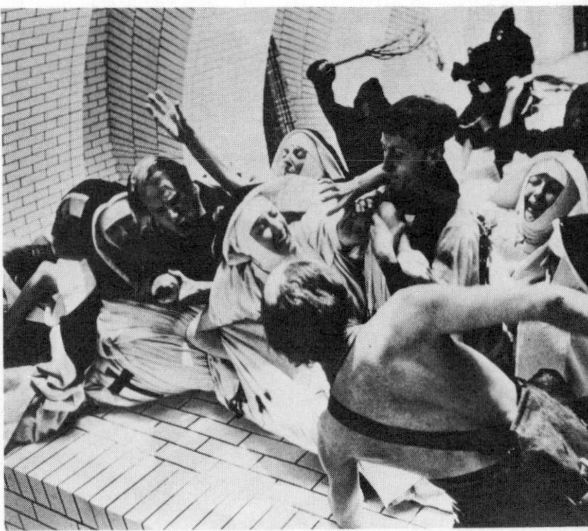

The torture of the possessed nuns in Ken Russell's *The Devils* (1971).

A suspected witch put to the question in *The Witchfinder General* (1968).

secutors of the deranged. Ken Russell's *The Devils* may be exaggerated and baroque in style, but it overblows the true story of Urbain Grandier, the ruler-priest of Loudun condemned to the stake because of denunciation by tortured nuns possessed with devils. Religious mania is still at the back of some of our cults of horror.

The Renaissance also led to a new theme in men's fantasies, the Age of Discovery. The little galleons and carracks of Europe were pushing out over the monstrous deeps to trade with and colonize the world. Early mapmakers peopled the deeps with huge monsters, just as early astronomers had seen monsters in the constellations. As grids and lines were drawn across the seas and the heavens, so the old beliefs in monsters still lurked in the deeps and flew the skies. Travellers' tales of weird beings in the oceans or dragons on land lingered on to become *The Creature from the Black Lagoon* and the uncompleted *Gwangi*. The discovery of new continents kept alive the possibility of finding new superbeasts or lost prehistoric monsters.

Constellations drawn as beasts and chemical experiments in a celestial map of 1828.

The appearance of *The Creature from the Black Lagoon* (1954).

The Valley of the Gwangi was never completed, but sequences and drawings remain.

The frontispiece of Hobbes's *Leviathan.* The King is meant to rule and contain all his subjects within the corporate state.

As the pace of scientific invention accelerated, so the idea of a controllable universe grew. In political philosophy, Hobbes took over the idea of Newtonian physics to formulate a theory of the corporate state, which he named after a monster, *Leviathan.* The agricultural revolution persuaded many people that animals and men could be bred to any size, something satirised by Jonathan Swift in *Gulliver's Travels* and featured in many a photo-montage and film of fantasy. But above all, the industrial revolution changed the concentration of the time to mechanical thinking. By the end of the 18th century, Adam Smith was talking of Economic Man, not of social or political or godly man. And the leading theory in British philosophy was Utilitarianism; in it, only what was useful was prized. The "dark Satanic mills" of William Blake were not seen for their infernal qualities, but for their profits. Although new fantasies were being created, particularly by the steam-engine that could power the train and the ship, they were fantasies of transportation, mechanical dreams.

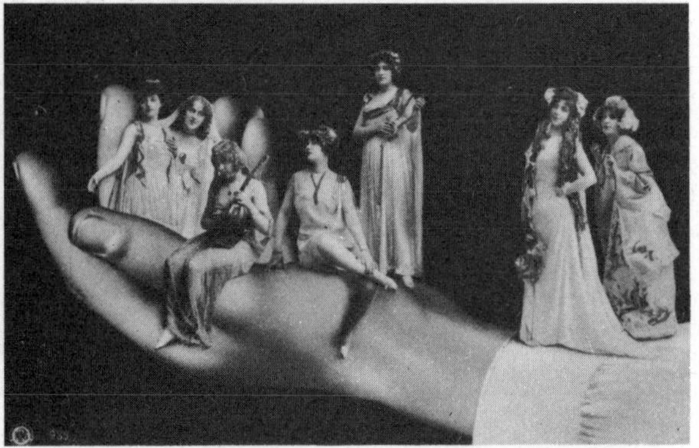

A French fantasy postcard, about 1900.

Kathryn Grant is held in the hand of the Prince of Bagdad in *The Seventh Voyage of Sinbad* (1958).

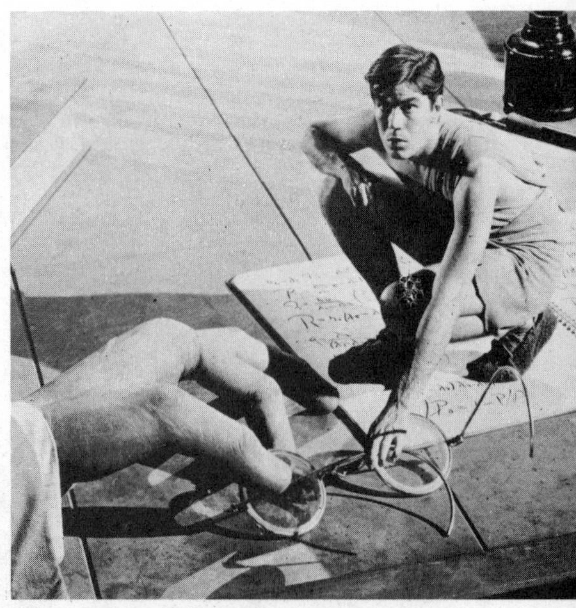

Dr. Cyclops' lenses are stolen by one of his miniature victims.

Against this mechanistic thinking, a romantic revolt was spawned. Its leader was William Godwin, the anarchist philosopher and father of Mary Shelley. He inspired both Percy Bysshe Shelley and Lord Byron with his radical ideas on the individual. William Blake, Wordsworth, and Coleridge were the first poets of the romantic revolution. Blake too painted along with Fuseli some of the apocalyptic visions that were to inspire the dream images of later times. Meanwhile, "Monk" Lewis and others were writing Gothic novels with their backgrounds of gloomy abodes, dark forests, ghosts and doom. Their evocation of eerie decor was to become a staple of the supernatural film epitomised in James Whale's *The Old Dark House* or in the brilliant British *Dead of Night*. The device of gathering together a few misshapen souls to tell fearful stories in a Gothic ruin or an isolated mansion was created by late Georgian Gothic writers and acted out in the meeting of the children of the romantic revolt in the Villa Diodati after the final defeat of Napoleon's attempt to rule the world.

John Henry Fuseli's painting *The Nightmare*, 1782. Fuseli was Byron's favourite painter.

Murder in the mirror in *Dead of Night* (1945).

The gothic atmosphere of *The Old Dark House* (1932).

It is possible to say that Lord Byron and Mary Shelley created the film of the supernatural in 1816. Percy Bysshe Shelley had eloped to Switzerland with Godwin's daughter, Mary, and also with Godwin's daughter by his first wife, Claire Clairmont, who was already Byron's mistress. They spent a summer by Lake Geneva. They talked endlessly of the controversies of the time, whether man's nature was savage or good before society transformed it, and whether electrical experiments could revive the dead and discover "the principle of life." Shelley had been brought up on ancient books of chemistry and magic which he read "with an enthusiasm of wonder, almost amounting to belief." Byron was already the romantic Devil-figure of Europe, an aristocrat proud of scandal and incest, a dabbler in revolution and a poet of lechery. Mary Shelley was fascinated by both her volatile husband Percy and his

Valerie Hobson as Elizabeth Frankenstein is terrified by the monster created by her husband.

friend Byron, who was certainly the most notoriously wicked man alive. Out of their suggestions, she created *Frankenstein.* In James Whale's second film on this subject, *The Bride of Frankenstein* of 1935, Mary begins the film by chatting with Shelley and Byron, who reproaches her for writing a monster tale.

"My purpose," she says, "was to write a moral lesson, of the punishments that befell a mortal man who dared to emulate God." The book falls in the fire, the film begins. Originally, Whale wanted the same woman to play both the actual wife of Count Frankenstein and the mate created by him for the monster, but in the end, Valerie Hobson played Elizabeth Frankenstein and Elsa Lanchester played the monster's mate, who also rejected and drove the monster to another orgy of destruction by fire. Whale's second Frankenstein film is the only version which sticks closely to Mary Shelley's original thinking and

Elsa Lanchester, as the mate created for the monster, rejects her loathsome love-to-be.

brings out the ambiguities of her concept, that illuminates so many of the dominant obsessions of her time and past times. As a contemporary review said: "Here is one of the productions of the modern school in its highest style of caricature and exaggeration. . . . There was never a wilder story imagined; yet, like most of the fictions of this age, it has an air of reality attached to it, by being connected with the favourite projects and passions of the times."

So Mary Shelley began the Frankenstein saga by amalgamating many of the strands of obsession which ran back to human prehistory and personifying them in the figures of the Faustian scientist Count Frankenstein and the bewildered monster of his creation that has come to bear his name. At the same time, one of her inspirers, Lord Byron, began and Polidori concluded a tale of vampires about a Lord Ruthven, as impeccable and English as any Basil Rathbone, who lived on the blood of his victims. This also started a cycle of novels and later films that remains the basis of much of our mass imagery today.

At Lake Geneva in 1816, the themes of the monsters and the scientists and the destructive lust for knowledge were linked in figures that still haunt us now.

Boris Karloff, as Frankenstein's monster, rages in the gothic graveyard of James Whale's film.

MACHINES

As terrible as the birth of Frankenstein's monster to the new day was the birth of the industrial revolution. At the same time as the freak made by invention was forcing his master to make him a mate, so the weavers were attacking the new machines that were to destroy their old way of life. The Luddites were trying to smash up the new Molochs of the factories that were to put them to toil and trial until death. But the machines conquered the old crafts and the cities grew and the words of progressive thinkers came to be the propaganda of

In Fritz Lang's *Metropolis* (1926), the workers in the underground city are treated as prisoners, while the giant machine they service has the face of Moloch, a mechanical giant of fire.

A Victorian cartoon on the follies of mesmerism or hypnotism.

the new industrialism. The romantics who attacked the engines of change at the time of Napoleon ended by worshipping them by the death of Queen Victoria. The lampooned cult for mesmerism, for seeing dream pictures in a hypnotic trance, was to be turned by a device into the truth. The fear of the machine turned into the fantasy of the machine. The monster enthralled his maker. There seemed no limits to the frontiers of knowledge. All progress was possible, and good. The age that began with riots against the machine ended by creating a dream machine, the cinema.

In his important book, *Archaeology of the Cinema*, Ceram points out that the cinema was not invented by the early suggestions of mirror writing and the automaton theatres of Heron of Alexandria, nor by the optical effects of Ptolemy, nor by the camera oscura of Alhazen, nor even by the strange lines of Lucretius on "moving pictures". The optical shows of the 18th and 19th centuries, the Dioramas and Panoramas, were also not film, nor were the moving slides in magic lanterns, although the Belgian Robertson could produce ghosts by this method. The principle of the persistence of vision was discovered by Plateau in a device made in 1832 called the Phenakisticope; at the same time, Stampfen invented the Stroboscope. They were basically slotted discs which were rotated in front of a mirror and showed twelve or more slightly different images of a bird flying or of a man running. Later Horner's Zoetrope mounted the band of pictures inside a revolving drum, where they could be seen through slots. The principle of a strip of pictures to give an illusion of movement was born. This principle is still the basic principle of the animated film, where a strip of pictures with slight changes of movement is usually projected at twenty-four frames a second past our eyes. The magic of *Pinocchio* or *The Little Island* is a mechanistic magic, developed from a theory and a toy.

A contemporary drawing of Robertson's experiments in the early 19th century.

A drawing from Walt Disney's *Pinocchio* (1939), followed by the final cartoon as Jimmy Cricket floats down the eye of the whale.

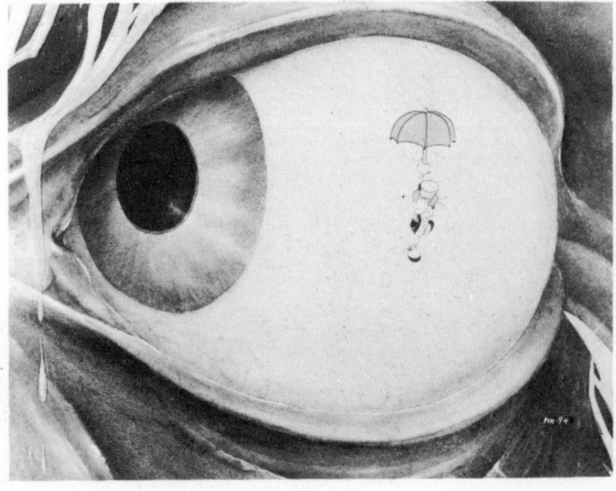

At the same time as the picture strip, the process of photography was developed in France by Niepce and Daguerre and Bayard. By the middle of the 19th century, there were portrait studios in every major European city. The Civil War photographs of artists such as Brady became the basis for scenes in later films such as *Gone With The Wind*. But photography only re-

The ruins of Richmond, Virginia, photographed by Brady in 1865.

The burning of Atlanta, Georgia, from *Gone with the Wind* (1939).

corded. It did not move, until the Californian Muybridge set twenty-four cameras side by side, triggered off by twenty-four threads across a race-track, to prove whether a galloping horse ever had all four legs off the ground. Muybridge's "series pictures" of humans and animals in motion were the first film strip, and their quality makes them a model for modern artists.

Three sequence studies of a nude model by Muybridge, first published in 1901.

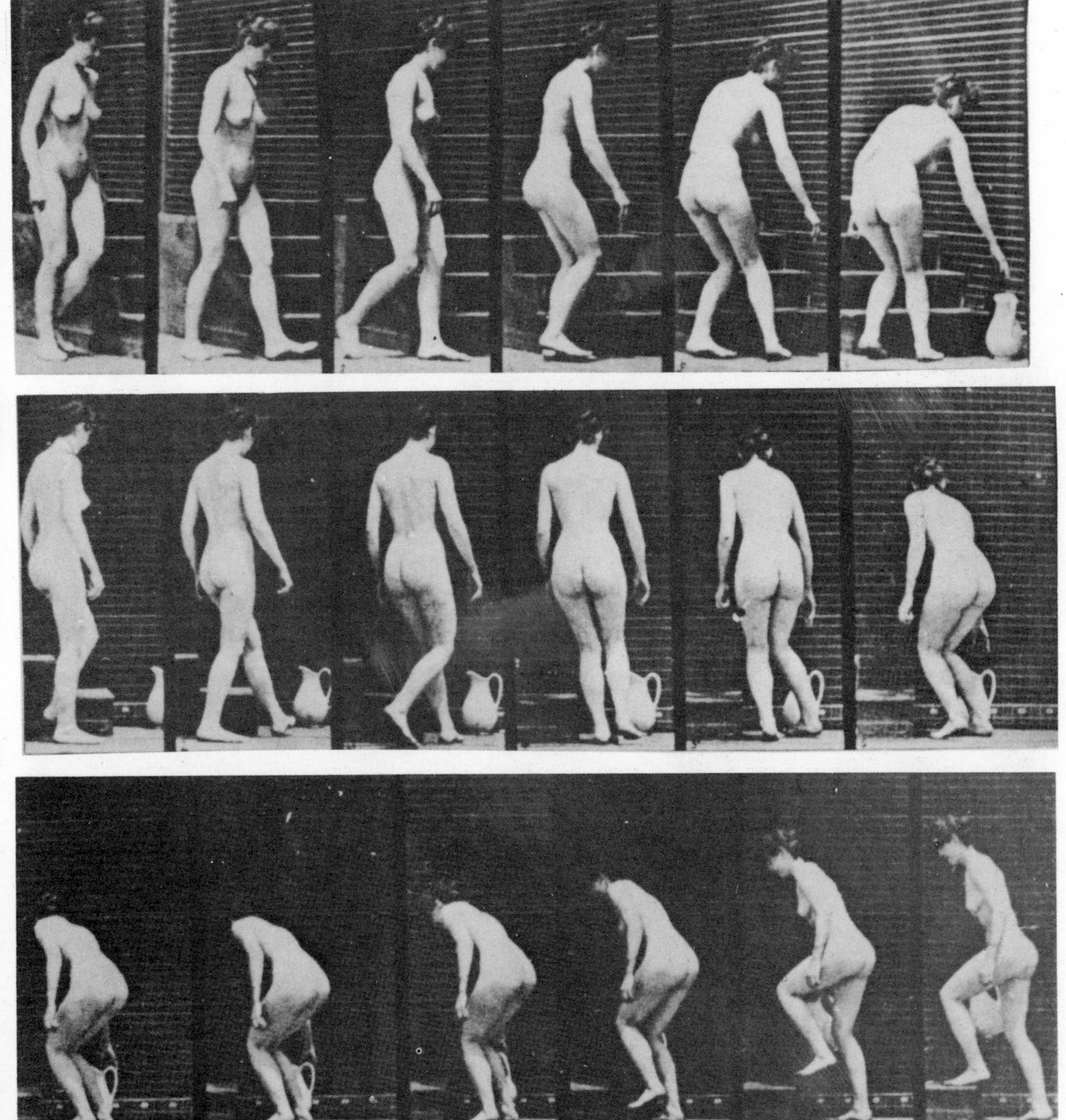

A woman walks towards camera in the Lumières' *L'arriveé d'un train en gare* (1895).

A contemporary picture postcard.

Afterwards, Eastman, with his roll of film and Edison with his Kinetograph camera and Kinetoscope viewer, invented by 1889 the basic technology necessary for making motion pictures, except for the film projector. Many other inventors tried their hands at Bioscopes and Chronophotographoscopes and Klondikoscopes and Kineopticons and Phantasmagorias, but only the brothers Lumière created and manufactured the Cinematograph, a combined cine-camera and printer and projector. The name of their product became the name of the new industry and art, cinematography. Their first film was of their workers leaving their factory. By 1895, a paying audience could see a train rolling into a station. Its effect was to put into motion the photo-montage postcards of the time.

The early films of the Lumières, although realistic, were still magical to their audiences. Machines had now found a way of reproducing visual reality in another place at a later time. The very process was the realisation of a fantasy. It was a dream caused by electrical light and celluloid film and a claw and cogs and a lens and a strip of pictures projected at a speed which fooled the human eye. The machine was the miracle at first. The medium was, indeed, the message. Only later, with the fantasy films and staged tricks of Méliès and his imitators, did the cinema audience, grown matter-of-fact about the process of moving pictures, learn to distinguish between the realistic film and the film of magic. Curiously enough, it was the science fiction of Jules Verne, which popularised new inventions such as the Lumières' Cinematograph, that haunted the best of Méliès work. Fantasy left the machine for the magician.

In the fever for reading and speculating about impossible voyages that made Jules Verne so widely read, the fantasy postcard was also popular. Until the arrival of the telephone, the postcard was the normal way of communicating – the average French person sent fifteen postcards a year. The transportation cards look similar to early film stills and certainly influenced Lumière and Méliès and, later on, the surrealist film-makers such as Réné Clair in *Entr'acte*. At their most interesting, the postcards and cigarette cards foretold a communications future that the early cinema could not hope to duplicate. One series describing the year 2000 is delightful in its predictions of dictaphones and the telegraphic cinema and the chase after microbes, not to mention underwater artists, hydroplanes and snow buggies at the South Pole. Initially, the cinema only had to draw on the popular graphics of the time to turn itself into a mass art of the future.

Correspondance Cinéma-Phono-Télégraphique.

Un Hydroplane.

Un Paysage océanien.

La Chasse aux Microbes.

From a fantasy postcard series, about 1900.

This late Victorian fascination with motion and machines that was to invent cinematography is perfectly shown in *The Motograph Moving Picture Book* of 1898, which was an attempt at home movies. Toulouse-Lautrec himself drew its cover and it is full of pictures of trains and steam boats and traction engines that appear to move when a coloured transparency is laid over them and jiggled. The optical illusion of movement is hallucinating. Equally interesting is the choice of subjects other than machines to animate – a magic head, a cat and a black cherub, a volcano. The book perfectly mirrors the division between the cinema of Lumière and the cinema of Méliès, between the realist film and the magical film, that was always to divide movie critics and fans according to their preferences.

"The Traction Engine" from the *Motograph Moving Picture Book* of 1898.

"The Magic Head" from the same book.

The fantasy of transportation was, indeed, integral to Victorian thinking. To get into a train was to begin a weird voyage. The use of machines by Jules Verne and H. G. Wells as a method of reconnoitring outer space or the innards of the earth or lost worlds was merely an extension of the mechanical dream. It would have been as strange for a Polynesian pygmy to enter a steam engine as for a Victorian to step on a moon rocket, yet Verne's illustrations make his moon rocket look like a train compartment. It is significant that the first films made in France, both realist and magical, dealt with transport. The brothers Lumière filmed a train from Vincennes coming into a station, while Méliès filmed a trip to the moon. Motion in real life did, of course, suit the process of motion pictures.

A contemporary illustration from Jules Verne's *Voyage dans la lune.*

In Méliès' *Voyage dans la lune* (1902), the explorers enter a shell very similar to the one described by Verne, and they are shot by a huge gun straight into the eye of the man on the moon.

Unlike the industrialist Lumière, Méliès was an ex-magician who invented most of the early optical illusions which depended heavily on *drawn* sets and effects. He relied on the science fiction prose and illustrations of Jules Verne, but he vulgarised the detailed matter-of-fact qualities of the original. Sometimes Méliès' images are antiquated, as in the image of the Coach of Death in *The Merry Frolics of Satan;* sometimes silly, as in a sort of balloon-supported aerial train in *An Impossible Voyage;* sometimes futuristic, as in the pointed shell fired on *A Trip to the Moon.* Yet even such a clinically futuristic film as *Moon Zero Two* can call its lunar buggy "Moon Fargo", harking back to the nostalgic lost past of Wells Fargo and Ford's *Stagecoach,* which also provoked death from a hostile landscape.

Another illustration from Verne's book shows the moon rocket as a sort of train, to which Méliès was later to add balloons for humorous effect.

Méliès' vision of a moonman pushing the moon rocket off the edge of the moon really does turn the sublime into the ridiculous.

The moon buggy confronts its strange new environment in *Moon Zero Two* (1969).

The stagecoach rolls on over the western desert, as barren as the surface of the moon.

The technique of the postcard is exactly the same as that of Méliès.

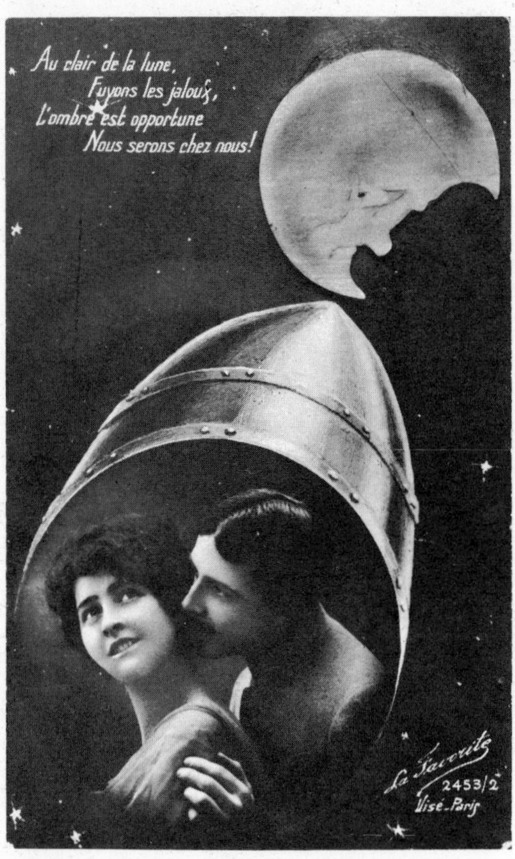

Au clair de la lune,
Fuyons les jaloux,
L'ombre est opportune
Nous serons chez nous!
La Favorite
2453/2
Visé_Paris

In all motion picture making, transportation has remained a mechanical dream. It is because the movie camera is itself a machine that moves to make a dream. By changing a cog, it can slow down or accelerate human action. By the close-up cut next to the long shot, it can make a standing jump of a mile from an object in one twenty-fourth of a second. It can play with speed and deny time. However realistic a film may be, the very process of its making is unreal in terms of human speed and human hours. It is the medium best adapted for portraying the mechanical dream, for that is the very process of film-making. A First World War postcard of a moon-shot may be animated by Méliès into half-drawing and half-photograph, then made by Lang as a huge studio set, then end as the documentary of an actual moon-shot. The effect on the watcher is much the same and creates exactly the same wish for a trip to the moon. It is the fantasy of escape through a practical machine that has fuelled dreams since the first days of the steam-engine and the moving picture.

The moon rocket is prepared for firing in Fritz Lang's *Woman on the Moon* (1928)

Apollo 11 on the launch pad at Cape Kennedy, the night before its Saturn rocket actually sent man off on his first successful journey to the moon.

The wish-fulfilment of speed and danger is also part of realistic films such as *Bullitt* and *The Italian Job* and *The French Connection*. Climactic car crashes and chases are not a part of the watchers' lives, but of their fantasies. And in those films, such as the James Bond series, where the hero keeps to an imaginary sort of reality in his various encounters with evil, the audience accepts cars that slant through alleys on one wheel or explosive gas pills that blow up the villain of *Live and Let Die* into a balloon larger than Méliès magical indiarubber head. There are few films outside Italian neo-realism which do not engage some fantasy of their audience in their plots, and the most common fantasy developed by the moving picture has been travelling dangerously.

Underwater exploration by machine has also been a favourite plunge into the subconscious. Jules Verne's Captain

Steve McQueen bounces his car over the hills of San Francisco in *Bullitt* (1968).

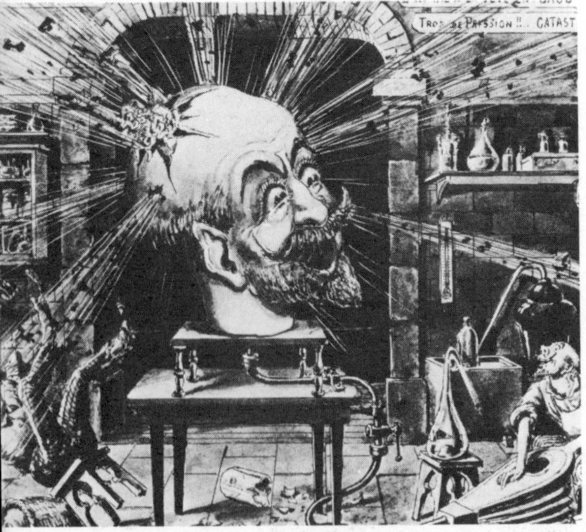

Méliès loved the trick of an expanding head and himself played the role of the swollen-headed magician.

Nemo revived the old Greek myth of the lost Atlantis, which had sunk back to that primeval time when a proto-human with gills first crawled out of the deep and could be presumed to be innocent. Both the machines of undersea exploration and of the moralities engage in journeys in the depths. In one scene in *Twenty Thousand Leagues Under the Sea*, aborigines attack the metal dragon-like Nautilus. *Fantastic Voyage*, however, proves the virtues of futurist medicine. In it, a miniaturised submarine is injected into a human vein to remove a blood-clot from a Very Important Person's heart; science fiction has sought its conscience below the surface. The world of Jacques Cousteau or of *The Neptune Factor* is not different, for the very tricks of underwater macrophotography can make a monster out of a shrimp and a model.

An animated *Nautilus* explores the depths in *The Fabulous World of Jules Verne* (1961).

Captain Nemo's men struggle with gigantic sea-monsters in *Twenty Thousand Leagues Under the Sea* (1954).
The *Nautilus* also repels a punitive attack.

The miniaturised submarine carrying surgeons drifts through the arteries of the Very Important Person in *Fantastic Voyage* (1966).

More fantastic to the Victorians than tales of the sea-bed were the stories of early travels in Africa. The explorations of Burton and Speke and Baker and Stanley and Livingstone opened the possibilities of finding a lost valley of prehistoric creatures, perhaps in the aptly named Mountains of the Moon. The urge to discover and plant the flag was an obsession of the time that was to push ambitious men on to travel in space. As Cecil Rhodes said, he "would colonise the planets if he could".

With the explorers travelled the scientists. Darwin's voyage in *The Beagle* to the South Seas and his discovery of the bones of dinosaurs and other gigantic creatures led him towards the theory of evolution. It is no accident that the greatest of the monster films, *King Kong*, begins with the arrival of a small ship at a lost Polynesian island. There the crew find Kong's jungle, where the mighty ape battles for supremacy with pterodactyls and dinosaurs and brontesauri. Likewise, Conan Doyle set his *The Lost World* in South America, where Professor Challenger led his explorers to a neanderthal age. While areas of the earth remained

King Kong fights to the death with his rivals (and over page).

unknown to Europe and America, they could be inhabitated by the monsters of prehistory or dream. It is only when the limits of the known world grew to cover the globe that monsters had to come again from under the seas or from space, like *Gorgo* or *The Beast From 20,000 Fathoms*. In the present days of space travel that prove there are no freaks on the moon which we do not send there, the monster of Loch Ness still remains possible, and the Japanese have even hunted the mythical giant serpent in a miniature submarine.

Gorgo destroys bridges and cities (and over page).

The classical idea of the eternal flame which is the source of everlasting youth also burned again in Rider Haggard's imaginative classic of African fiction and exploration, *She*. The renewal of the Queen through purification by fire is another use of the myth embodied in the Olympic torch and in the Wagnerian legends of a queen lying asleep in a circle of flame. *She* has remained one of the staples of fantasy movies and has been made often,

In this early version of *She* (1934), youth is renewed in the sacred fire.

although the basic idea has seldom been reduced as low as in *Fire Maidens From Outer Space*, which even harks back to Méliès' worst theatrical habit of lining up chorus girls to show their legs before starting his version of Verne's journey to the moon. The theme of the fire-maidens even comes into the last and best section of Walt Disney's *Fantasia*, where three flame sprites turn on the Devil's hand into the shapes of a pig, a wolf and an ass.

The mystic renewal by flame from *Fire Maidens from Outer Space* (1956), starring Susan Shaw.

Méliès' chorus-line of moonshot artillery girls and mermaidens was the forerunner of the Mack Sennett bathing beauties.

The Morlocks attack Rod Taylor in *The Time Machine* (1960).

Yet all Méliès' use of Verne's novels was not connected directly with the cinema in the way that H. G. Wells was through his book, *The Time Machine*. Wells had met the pioneer of the English cinema, Robert Paul, and they applied in 1895 to take out a patent for a Time Machine which would give those who entered it the illusion of travelling backwards and forwards through the

Although Robert Paul's short films were generally realistic, he was also capable of the effects of a Méliès, as in *The Magic Sword* (1902).

ages. It was to have retractable walls and floors, screens for slides and films, wind vents and special effects. Nothing came of the idea, for Wells returned to concentrate on his writing in a period that was to be wonderfully fertile for cinema ideas. Paul, however, pursued his researches, but he was too far ahead of his age, and he had no brilliant entrepreneur like Pathé to back him.

In a period just before the turn of the century, Wells continued to write many of the themes of later science fiction, the techniques of surgical transplantation in *The Island of Doctor Moreau*, the optical illusions of *The Invisible Man*, the planetary struggle of *The War of the Worlds*, and the little monsters of *First Men in the Moon*. If Mary Shelley's *Frankenstein* and Byron's and Polidori's

Claude Rains plays the *Invisible Man* (1933).

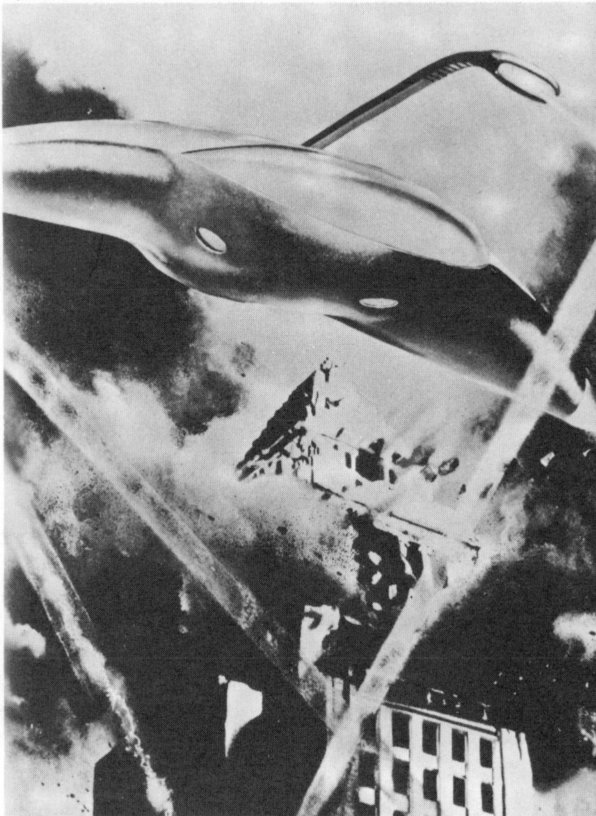

Catastrophe strikes the earth in *The War of the Worlds* (1953)

Harryhausen again did the special effects for *First Men on the Moon* (1964).

The Vampire synthesised most of the myths of later science fiction at the beginning of the 19th century and of the Romantic Revolt against the Machine, then Jules Verne and H. G. Wells synthesised most of the late Victorian romantic involvement with the Machine. In that time of fervent belief in mechanical progress, nothing that a machine could do seemed really evil. A mechanical invention such as the camera and the cinema projector itself seemed only able to benefit mankind. The ambiguities of the Frankenstein monster and of the Golem were forgotten in the search to conquer distance and time and labour. When the planet was freshly opened to exploitation and the use of man, why worry about the dull evil possible in a machine in bad hands? Not until the holocaust of the First World War was the possibility of total destruction by air and land and sea machine, by bomber and tank and battleship, made real to futurist writers and film-makers. Until then it was an elegant game of toys, fantastic and unreal.

A First World War French postcard of German atrocities.

Two pre-First World War postcards of futurist machines which were expected to fight in wars in the year 2000.

Myths

Au clair de la lune,
Nous irons s'il faut,
Jusqu'à Pampelune,
Bâtir des châteaux!

La Favorite
2453/4
Visé_Paris

Machines

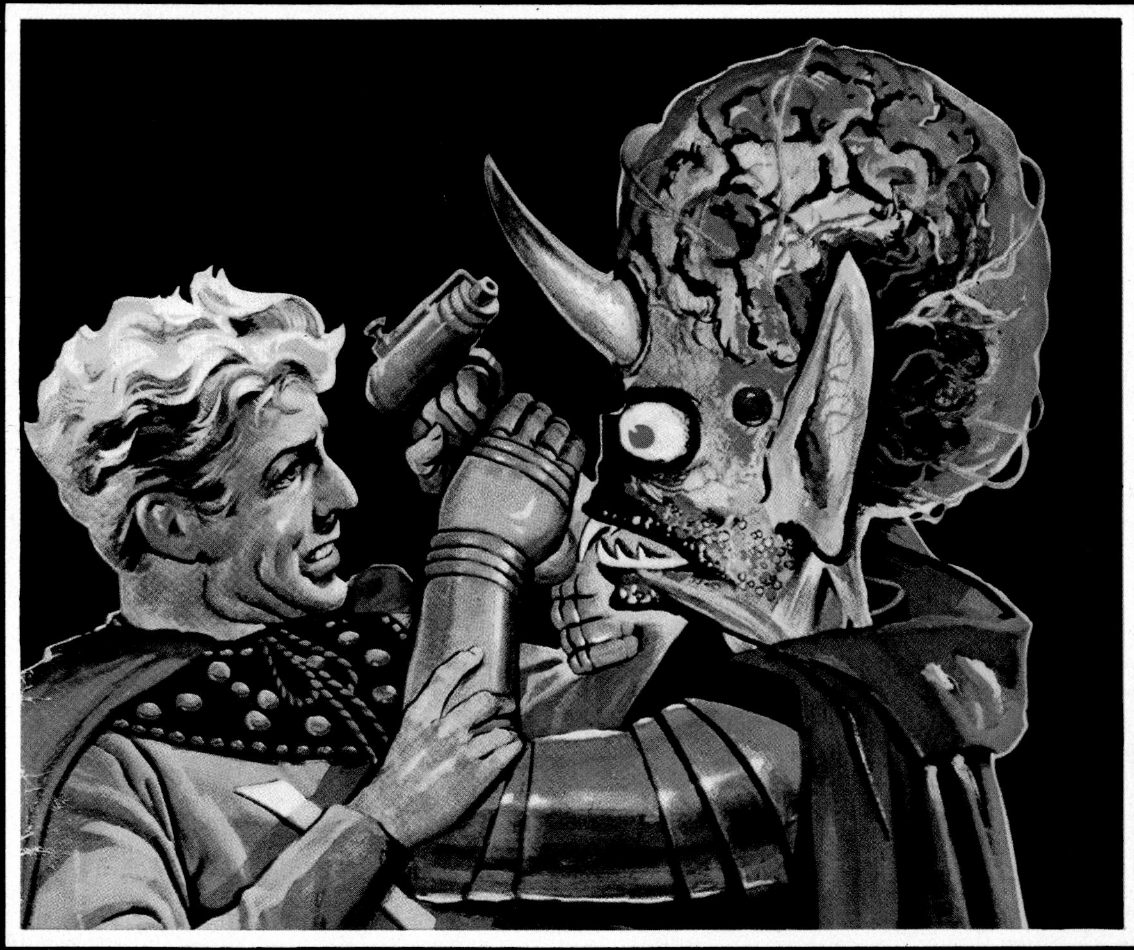

Visions

VISIONS

The discovery of psychiatry and the First World War changed men's view of fantasy. The motives behind a belief in myths and monsters began to appear. The outer fears of giants and demons were revealed as the inner fears of mankind, large on the heavens or the cinema screen. Meanwhile, the easy belief in mechanical progress of the late Victorians became fouled with the massacres and horrors created by the industrialism that produced the conscript armies, which died in front of the machine-guns and barbed-wire and tanks of the First World War. As the monster of mythology diminished to the disorderings within each man's body, so the useful machine grew into the bronze giant destroyer of the Greeks, Talos the Sardinian, who embraced his enemies with his burning hug and smiled his sardonic grin. If dragons were now the toys of the subconscious, the creatures of Haephestus or Count Frankenstein actually razed and killed men in their millions. The fear of the unknown lessened, the fear of the machine grew. The great beast was now the product of human invention.

The first classic fantasy films date from the First World War and Germany. With the collapse of the war machine, so horrifically shown in Pabst's later *Westfront 1918*, the Ger-

The German attack in Pabst's *Westfront 1918*, made in 1930.

man cinema turned back to its old mythology and the dark roots of its culture. In *The Cabinet of Dr. Caligari*, the world itself is distorted by the vision of a demonic doctor who raises up the hypnotised Conrad Veidt, the most beautiful of film humanoids, to kill for him in a maniac vision of power. This great masterpiece of the fantasy cinema was accompanied by two others, the second version of the *The Golem* and *Nosferatu*. Paul Wegener as the monster Golem represents the power of the war machine that turns back on its own creators to destroy them. Max Schreck as the original Dracula carries his coffin as if he would bury a whole generation in it, which has starved to death as he has from lack of blood. The collapse of Germany led to a flight from film reality, a seeking in legend for the auto-destruction of a society.

This Germanic school of fantasy film-makers was influenced both by an art of distortion called Expressionism, and also by the excesses and despairs of the early days of the German Republic. Expressionism had grown up before the Great War, while necrophilia and an ornate ghoulishness had always been part of national tradition from the ancient catacombs of Hallstatt to the

Conrad Veidt is resurrected from his box and carries off the sacrificial maiden over distorted roof-tops, past metal tangles which look like barbed wire, in *The Cabinet of Dr. Caligari* (1919).

Paul Wegener plays his seminal role as *The Golem* in the 1920 version.

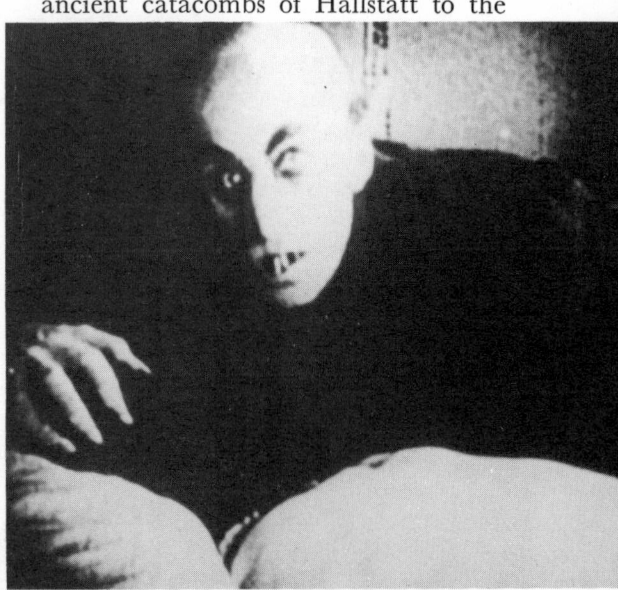

Max Schreck is the most spare and eerie of all the Draculas in *Nosferatu* (1922).

KOKOSCHKA

OK

DRAMA-KOMOEDIE
SOMMERTHEATER IN DER
KUNSTSCHAU
REGIE-ERNST REINHOLD

DRUCK VON ALBERT BERGER WIEN VIII. TIGERG. 17

A poster by Oskar Kokoschka, 1907.

The catacombs of Hallstatt in Upper Austria have been tenanted for thousands of years.

The shadowy world of *Dr. Mabuse* (1922).

works of Kokoschka and Nolde. The great fantasy creations of the early Germanic cinema not only dealt with horror, but with the ancient Wagnerian legends and the manipulations of super-criminals. Lang worked through *Destiny* and *Siegfried* and *Kriemhild's Revenge*, depicting a chiaroscuro world of magic light and dark, before he showed an equal mastery of the shadow-world of international crime in his films about Dr. Mabuse, rightly called by the great Lotte Eisner, "less of a superman than a product of the inflation period, a kind of tireless Proteus".

Yet even Lang never approached the incredible sorcery of Murnau's *Faust*, where Mephisto holds a whole city in his cloak and sweeps German cinema into demonic dreams far more rich and misshapen than the drunken distortions of people seen by the doorman in *The Last Laugh* – a technique Lang was to exploit the following year in his own *Metropolis*. The grotesque paintings of the Expressionists had become actualised in the magic of the cinema, which had learned to deal with the strange visions of man suffering from paranoia or alcohol or delirium of grandeur. The inner warping of men had been translated by special lenses into an outer vision of a misshapen world. The dream machine of the cinema had learned to portray the fears of men.

The actual technique of the cinema is one of exaggeration and distortion. The lens and the dream machine cause unreality and monstrous effects. As early as 1900, the Englishman G. A. Smith made *A Big Swallow*. In this film, an open mouth was brought closer and closer to the spectator until it seemed to gulp him down – the earliest version of trick audience inclusion that was to progress through the triple screens of Abel Gance's *Napoléon* to the roller-coaster ride in *This is Cinerama*. The close-up became part of the director's technique, particularly when the Rus-

Siegfried rides through the huge studio forest on a white horse as magical and contrived as any Fuseli nightmare, to discover the treasure of the Nibelungs.

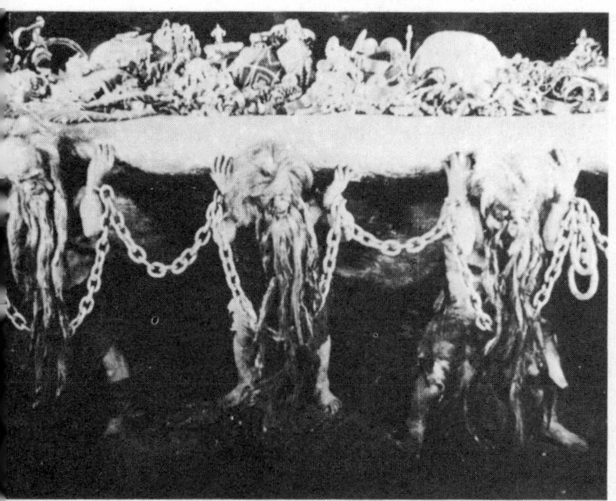

In *Kriemhild's Revenge* (1923–24), we see the contrast of innocence with the spirit of total destruction exemplified by the Mongol leader.

The Devil bestrides all in *Faust* (1926).

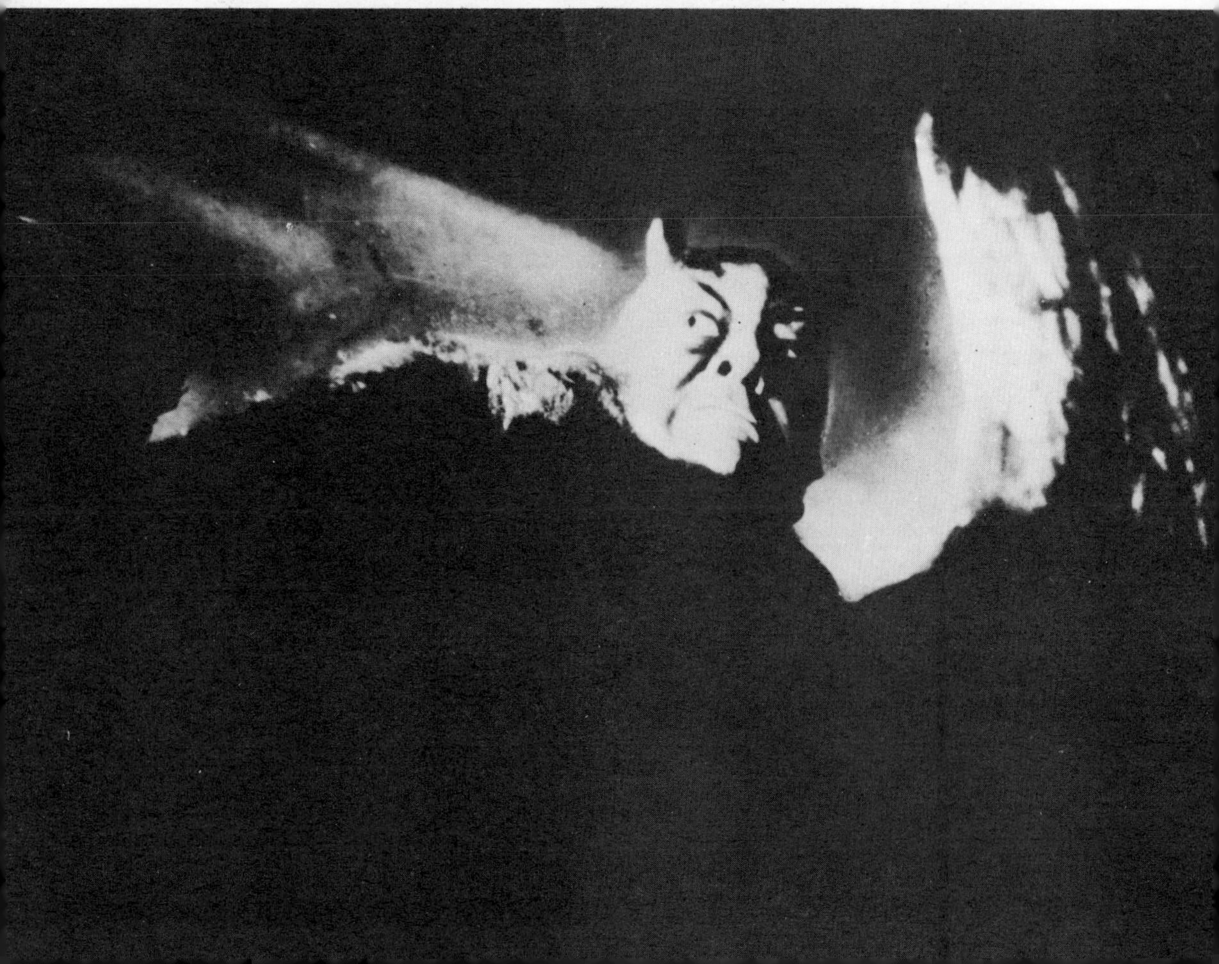

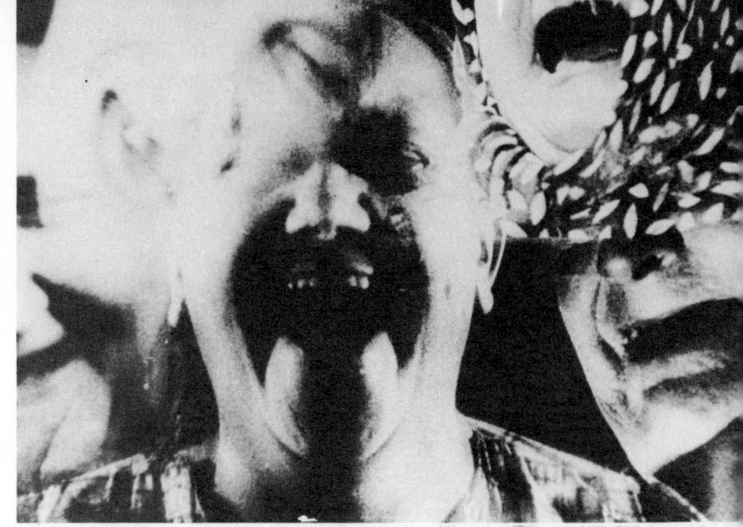

The optical effects achieved by Murnau in *The Last Laugh* (1924), showed the possibility of a cinema which examined subjective distortion and emotion.

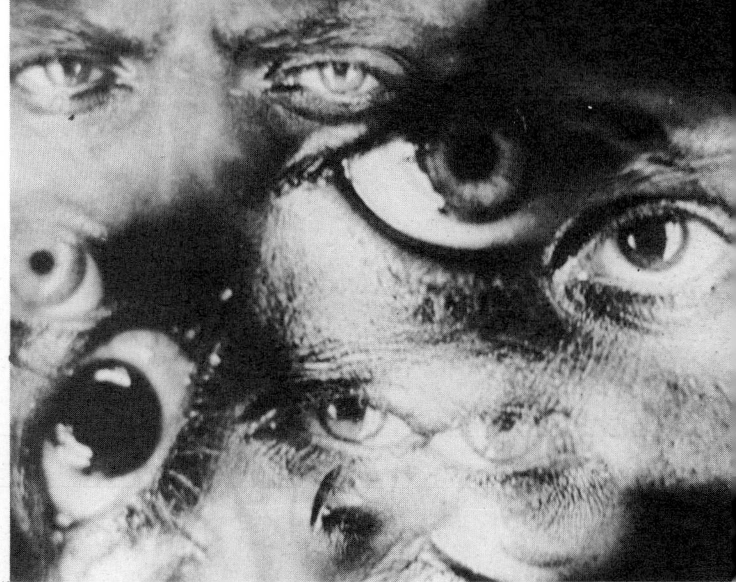

Fritz Lang's use of superimposition in *Metropolis* (1926) also extended the possibilities of the cinema.

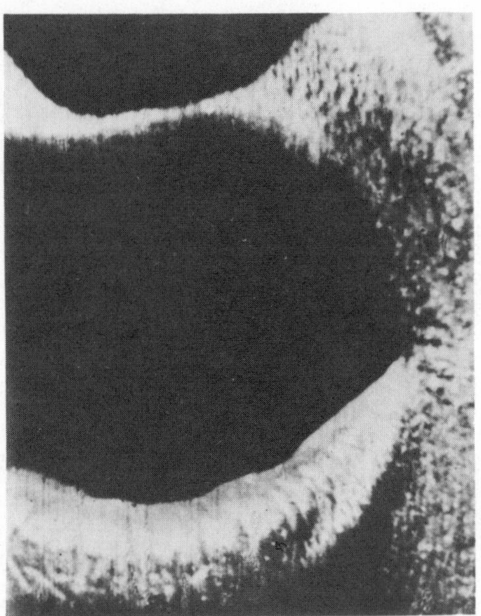

Part of the mouth for *A Big Swallow* (1900).

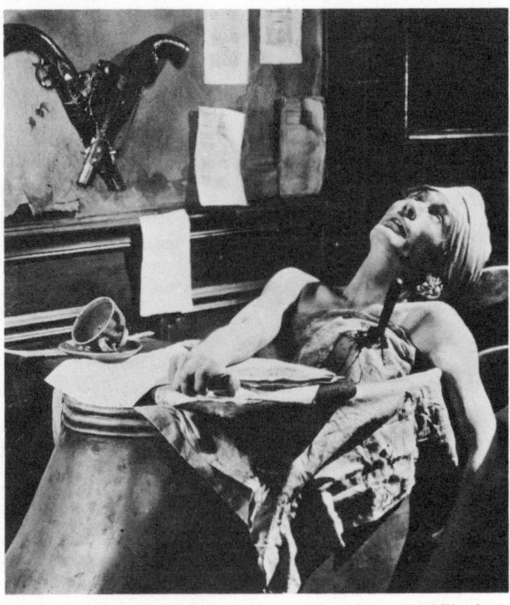

Abel Gance's immensely long *Napoleon* (1927), is technically so advanced that it is rarely shown because of projection difficulties.

The pram in the Odessa steps sequence in *The Battleship Potemkin* (1925).

sian directors after the Bolshevik Revolution introduced quick editing to create a crescendo as in the Odessa Steps sequence of *The Battleship Potemkin*, where the falling pram is as ghostly and mocking as any Coach of Birth and Death.

Size of image and speed of action became the magic of even the realist cinema. And learning from Renaissance painters such as Uccello, Eisenstein and particularly Pabst discovered the art of using the foreshortened angle and the tilted camera to give impressions of strength or weakness, of anger or gentleness. In the angle of the shot was its mystery and its implication. The fantasy of the cinema lay in a technique which could conjure up by shadow and camera position a nightmare or a dream.

Pabst was the third of the great innovators of the Expressionist German cinema. Despite his evocative work in *The Loves of Jeanne Ney* and later in *The Threepenny Opera*, his erotic masterpiece of suggestion through atmosphere and angle is *Pandora's Box* (*Lulu*), where Louise Brooks becomes the epitome of casual evil. She is the provoker of crime through carelessness and dies at the hands of Jack the Ripper. Wedekind's play gives Pabst a free hand to exercise his genius at the tilted camera, so that the animal and impassive face of Louise Brooks can seem as strange and cold as the surface of the moon, while the low angle shots of Dr. Schön and Roderigo emphasise their male brutality and lessen their brains. Pabst's London of fog and shadow is the continental Dickensian myth that never was but here exists. To Wedekind's romantic plays of corruption, Pabst brought a camera and fantastic vision that has never been equalled. Through him, we can see how brittle is evil, how dark the other side of the light, how dangerous the knife-edge of respectability that rips up those who deny its point.

Louise Brooks moves from careless gaiety to despair in *Pandora's Box* (1928).

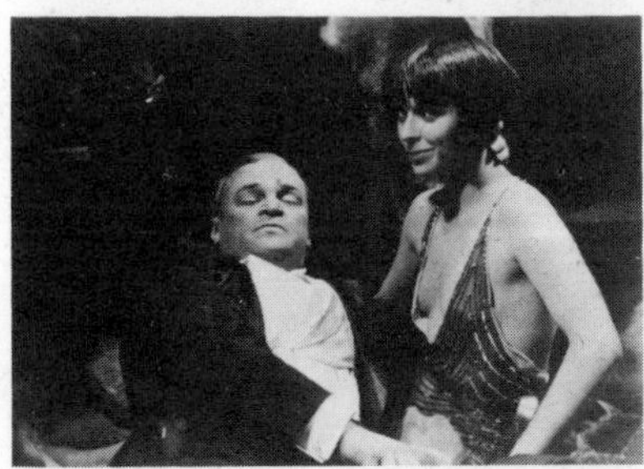

One film of the time, Arthur Robison's *Warning Shadows*, seems a neglected masterpiece that above all relates men's terrors to the first spooky shadows of childhood and to the origins of the dream machine. One of the earliest forms of moving picture was a shadowy play, where the fingers of an uncle with the light behind him could make rabbits, ducks or dragons magnify and move on the nursery wall. In Robison's *Warning Shadows*, the jealous husband first sees his wife in shadow-play with lovers – in fact, as the camera shows later, she is only surrounded by polite attentions. Robison's inspiration stems as much from nursery games as from Freud, for in the plot an illusionist (who is also the Devil) steals the shadows of the players and allows them to act out their secret fantasies. The shadow play is the truth of what real bodies repress. The masterpiece ends with the murder of the actual lover by the husband, and the illusionist riding away from the town like Satan on a pig. *Warning Shadows* is a seminal study for the fantasy cinema.

In *Warning Shadows* (1923), the shadows on the wall play out the motives and actions of the characters.

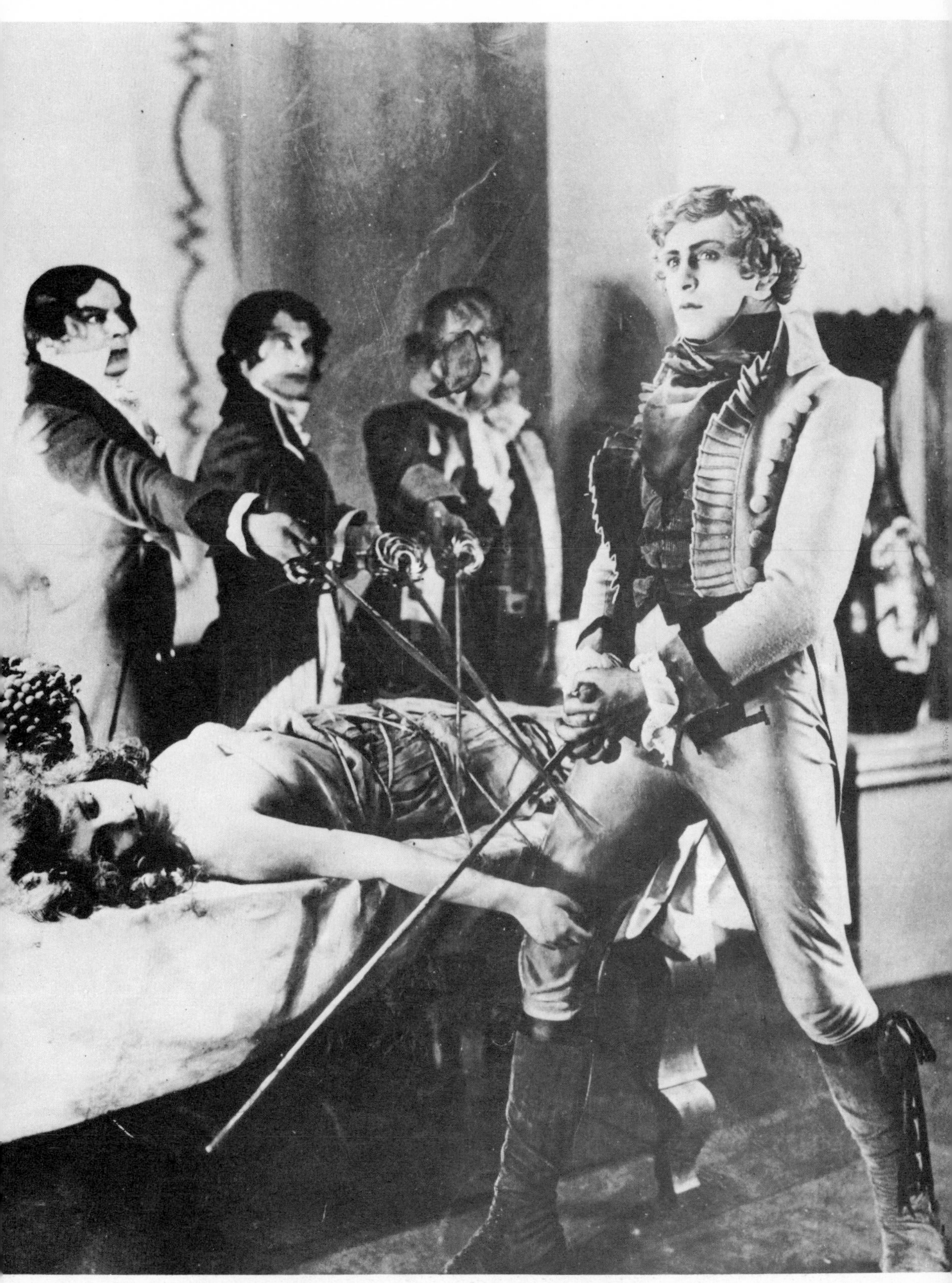

Lang is the most conscious user of mythology in *Metropolis*. He deliberately incorporates the images of legend into his futurist city.

Yet the genius of the German cinema could no longer continue denying the mechanical disaster of the First World War in groping for the dark shadows of corruption and the soul. Lang's pursuit of Wagner and the past ended with his unsurpassed prophecy in *Metropolis* of the machine and the future of mass man. The vision of the slaves toiling to build the Tower of Babel is replaced by the vision of the workers of Metropolis massing in revolt. The overground city is as intolerable as the underground city. Crowds of labourers mass on the cross of their work; their very bodies become the hands of the time clock which is also a furnace. Yet despite the functionalism of Lang's industrial perception, he remains steeped in the tradition of the alchemist. Rotwang's house is the last medieval cottage left among the girders. And when the underground city is flooded and the workers storm up to burn the mechanical Maria as a witch, the final climax traditionally takes place on the roof of the cathedral, to allow Lang to exercise his Gothic talents. *Metropolis* is the bridge between ancient myth and the machine world of mass man.

By the time Lang went on to make *Woman on the Moon*, the actual technique of a moon-shot obsessed him far more than any early efforts to resurrect old allegories. He could not do without his usual mad professor – a long way from a true rocketeer like Wernher von Braun who was later to aim at the moon even if he did sometimes hit London. Nor could Lang give up a lunar cavern straight from *Siegfried;* but his general documentary approach to the firing of the rocket was a technical triumph and an uncanny prediction of space flights to come.

Despite the last flickers of the classic German cinema in the shadowy *M* and the atmospheric *The Blue Angel* and *The Threepenny Opera*, the rise of the Nazis was to make mechanical the art of the

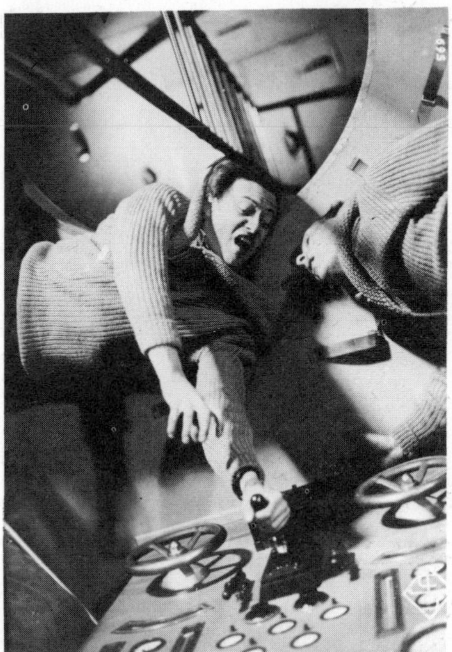

The moonshot sequences from *Woman on the Moon* (1928), were devised by a scientist already working on a future rocket programme which was to terminate in the V-1 and V-2.

dream machine in Germany. The sole Nazi classic is Leni Riefenstahl's *Triumph of the Will*, where men as massed machines perform their evolutions in chiaroscuro and worship of a Hitler, sometimes haloed for effect. The genius released in the German cinema by the revolt from the war machine was finally distorted in the service of that war machine rolling again.

The Russian cinema had already used men in mass action as shapes on the screen, crosses and circles of motion, in the work of Eisenstein and his contemporaries. Before the dull hand of Stalinist realism finally destroyed the fantastic element in the early Russian cinema, Eisenstein had explored the full possibilities of ritual even on a sequence about a collective farm and a milk machine, while his stooping shapes and misshapen vision in *Ivan the Terrible* are both more warped and magical and true than anything Sternberg could do in his exaggerated *The Scarlet Empress*. In the Stalinist state, Eisenstein had to turn to history in Ivan and Alexander Nevsky to find a lost age in which to indulge his rich and strange vision of the rituals and motions of men. The past can be as great an escape into fantasy as the future.

The glorification of the Nazis in *Triumph of the Will* (1934), shows the propaganda potential of the camera.

In *Ivan the Terrible* (1943–46), Eisenstein even persuaded his lead actor to walk in an exaggeratedly stooped way to fit the framing of each shot.

Hollywood Russia in *The Scarlet Empress* (1934) is both exaggerated and over-glamourised.

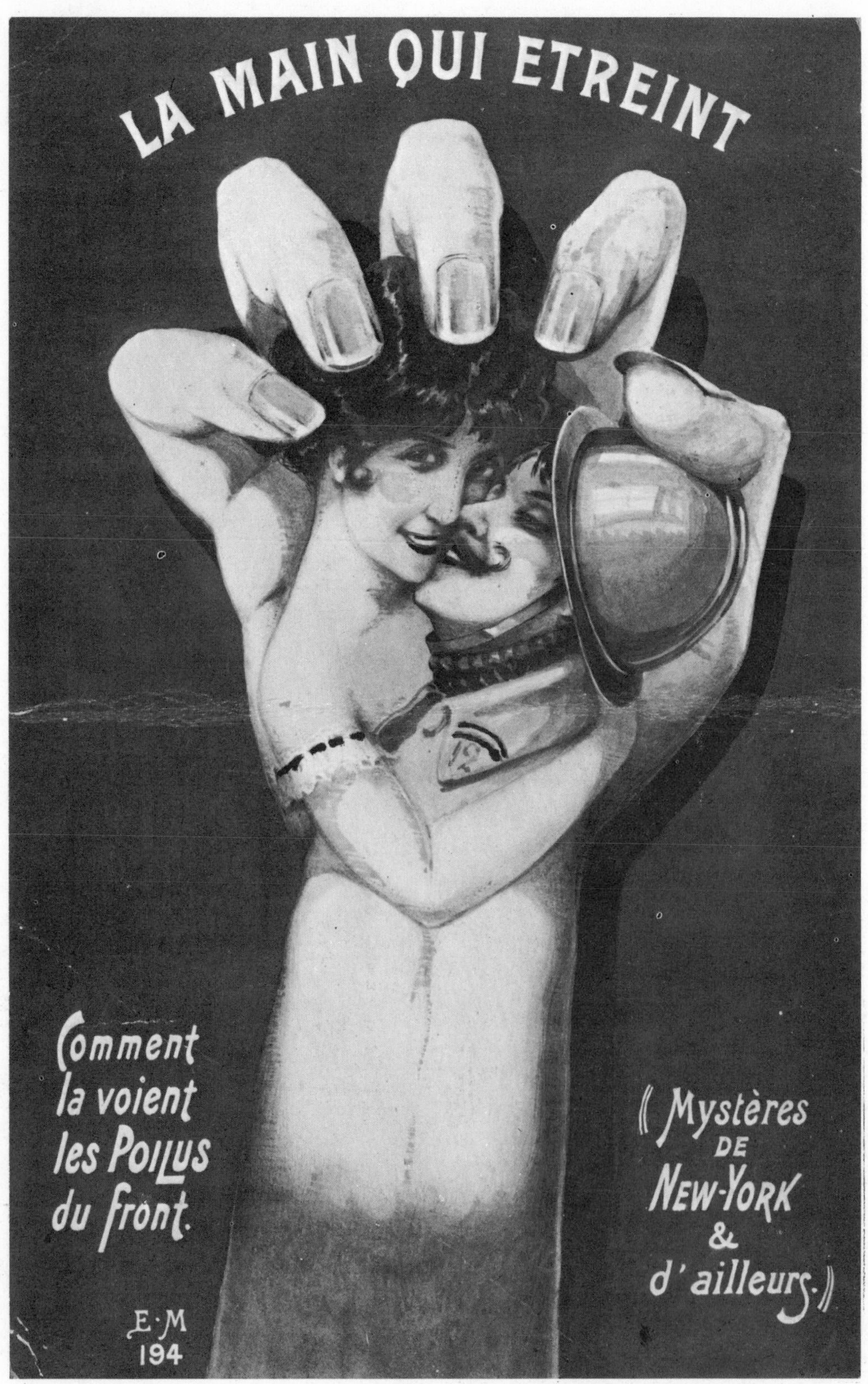

A First World War picture postcard.

In France, however, even the massacres of the First World War did not lead to a revolt from the romance of the machine. Fantasy postcards continued through the war, glamourising the mud and the horror, making out the trenches to be a sort of romance. And when the Armistice came, the French cinema did not seek its inspiration in the legends of Charlemagne. For Frânce was victorious. It still believed in progress. Its period of guilty soul-searching in the world of past ages came after its defeat in 1940. But for the moment, Abel Gance carried on the bold experimentation of Lumière and Méliès. In an early film, *The Madness of Dr. Tube*, Gance used concave and convex mirrors from an amusement park to show a distorted world through the eyes of a madman. Finally, he was to conclude his pioneer work with the triple split-screen effects of his masterpiece *Napoléon*, where effects of storms and ghosts overwhelm the audience and engulf them in the screen.

Generally, however, the French cinema pursued a realist line with its distinctive flavour captured in a fond look at the life of the streets. The films of the great Renoir after *The Match Girl* and of Réné Clair after *Entr'acte* shun exaggeration, as does most of the French cinema between the wars. *A Nous la liberté* with its futurist vision of a factory-made society has none of the grandiose terrors of a *Metropolis*. (The forcible mechanical feeding of Charles Chaplin, indeed, in *Modern Times* is far more horrific and prophetic of the age of the conveyor belt.)

In detail and humour the French cinema found its strength – except in surrealism. And here its cinematic genius was a Spaniard, Luis Bunuel, especially when his screenwriter was another Spaniard, Salvador Dali, in *The Andalusian Dog*. The images of that film from cut eyes to severed hands, to the hero dragging ropes tethered to priests, dead donkeys and grand pianos

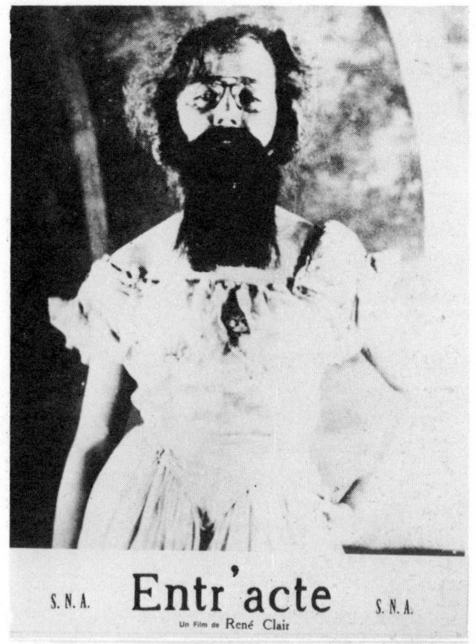

The crazy images of *Entr'acte* (1924) and the factory fantasies of *A Nous la liberté* (1931) show Clair at his most perceptive.

were more extravagant and horrific than any monster film of the time. The explicit eroticism of *The Andalusian Dog* and more particularly of its successor *The Age of Gold* was both savage and obviously Freudian. In the second film, the lover is shown sitting on a lavatory while lusting for his beloved. For the first time, Bunuel dared to show that excretion can be part of passion. The lover throughout behaves like a beast among the bourgeoisie. He shows his violent and Freudian urges and ends by smashing his surroundings like any monster of Frankenstein. These two early classics of surrealism invented a mysterious cinema of the psyche that ends in the obscene beauties of Jodorowsky's *The Mole*.

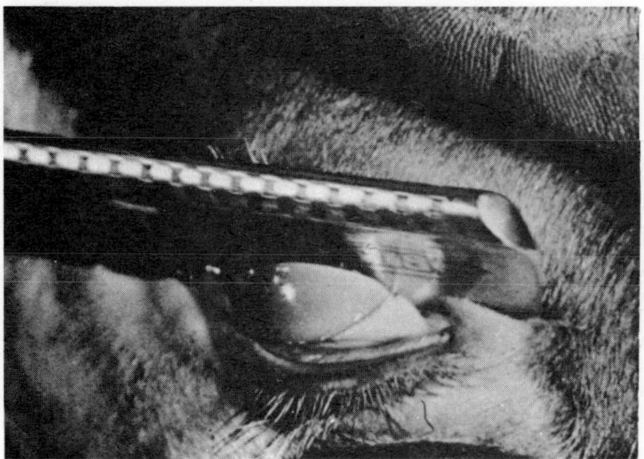

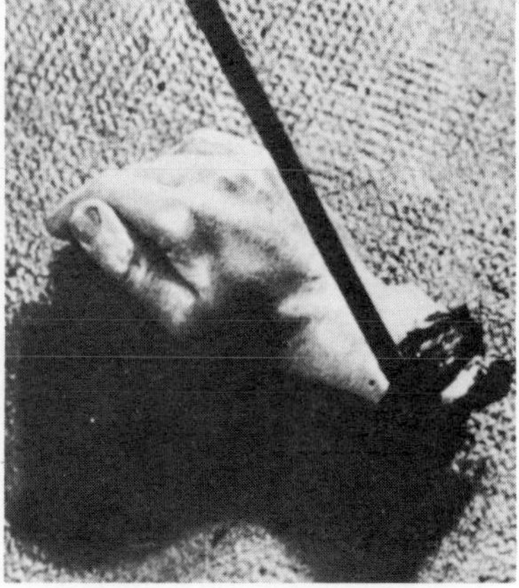

The images of *The Andalusian Dog* (1928) remain the most hallucinatory in the history of cinema.

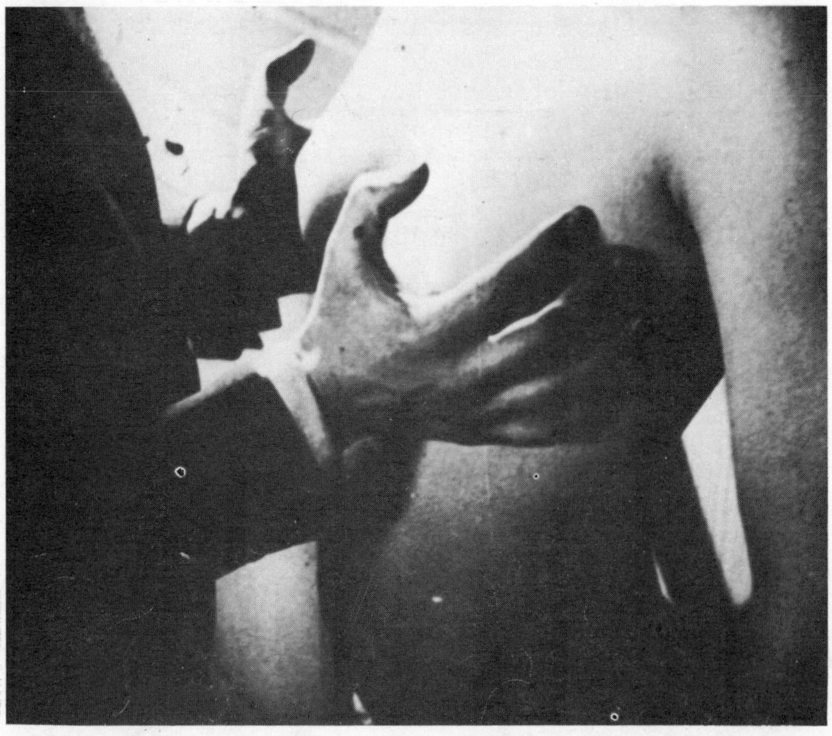

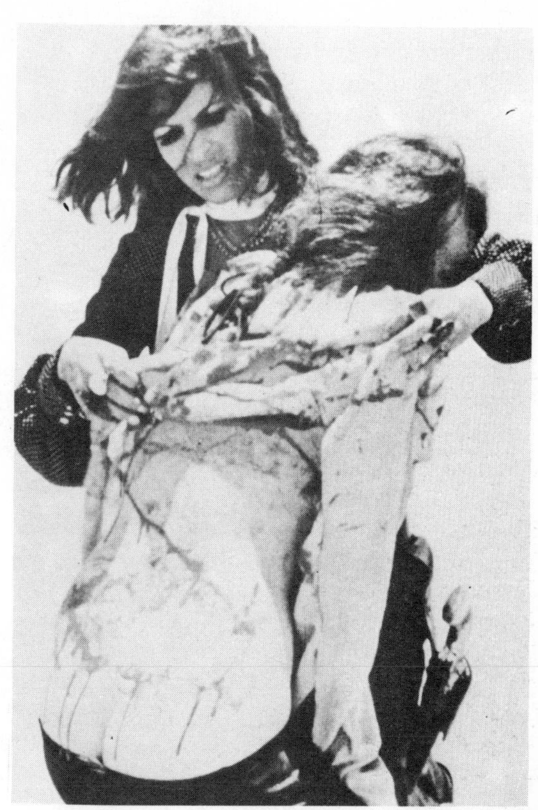

Jodorowsky's *The Mole* (1972) owes an enormous but unpaid debt to Bunuel.

In Britain, however, surrealism did not affect the cinema. The elements of fantasy in major British films between the world wars were industrial. While the irrepressible Méliès had first depicted the Channel Tunnel in 1907, Maurice Elsey showed a more workmanlike one in 1929 and a huge transatlantic one in 1935. His sets were almost as grandiose as Otto Hunte's remarkable futurist machines in *Gold*, which turned alchemy into a superfactory. But the culmination of mechanical dreaming came in 1936 in William Cameron Menzies' *Things to Come*, based on the old H. G. Wells irrepressible scientific optimism. In the film, a Second World War destroys all civilised cities and reduces London to ruins and barbarism, before a race of aerial technocrats rebuilds the world. By 2036, the underground city of Everytown has been built as the antithesis of Metropolis – it is light and open and terraced, lying under the green hills of the world above. And finally, despite a Luddite mob that rages at the restless inventors, a vast space gun is fired to probe the moon and the stars. The question is put, "All the universe – or nothingness?" If there is psychological doubt, the Frankenstein urge for the outer limits of knowledge even at the price of destruction must be satisfied, or else the human race will relapse into sloth and savagery. In the last years of the British Empire, a belief in Victorian progress was not yet dead. The planets would yet be colonised.

If mechanical dreaming ruled the British fantasy cinema, the American cinema engulfed all the fictions capable of appealing to the box-office – freaks and vampires, monsters and robots. In films of fantasy, there emerged two directors of genius, Tod Browning and James Whale, two extraordinary actors, Lon Chaney Sr. and Boris Karloff, and two masters of special effects, Willis

The sets in *The Tunnel* (1935) show the size of the stages in the large pre-war British studios.

O'Brien and Ray Harryhausen. Tod Browning knew the circus well and used it as a background in his earliest film, *The Unholy Three*, where Lon Chaney Sr. is a ventriloquist dressed as an old woman, who robs with a strong man and a midget dressed as a baby. In its sequel, *The Unknown*, Chaney is an "armless" knife-thrower (actually his arms and hands, one with two thumbs, are hidden in a straitjacket). He has his arms amputated for the love of a girl, Joan Crawford, and then arranges for her lover to be pulled apart by wild horses on a jammed revolving stage. Every terror of inner warping is expressed by outward amputation in *The Unknown* with a beautiful pathos shown by Chaney, who in one sequence ignores his hands and smokes a cigarette with his toes with such naturalness that he might have done so all his life. Yet this film was only Browning's prelude to his masterpiece *Freaks*, which was made after his hugely successful version of *Dracula* with Bela Lugosi. In *Freaks*, Browning does the impossible – he makes his audience grow to appreciate and love the misshapen and the dwarfed and the pin-headed and the mutilated. His collection of midgets and monsters from birth, not choice, became the unwished children of the audience, which is why the film was not successful. Browning's only mistake was to show the actual revenge of the freaks upon the silly beautiful Cleopatra who betrays one of them – she is cut down to a fowl with a human face. But the chant of the freaks to Cleopatra at the wedding feast, "One of us, one of us, one of us!" is the measure of Browning's cinematic genius. Alone, he makes us jump from revulsion to affection for the little monsters of our loins. There, but for the grace of God and the genes, crawl we.

Things to Come (1936) was the most grandiose film yet to be made in Britain. It was a critical and popular success and showed that the British industry could produce films on a Hollywood scale.

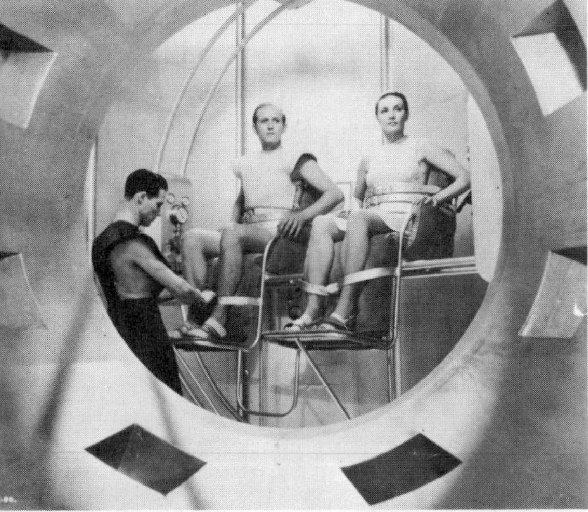

Lon Chaney Snr in *The Unknown* (1927), using his feet as hands.

Lugosi turned the weird Dracula of Schreck into the smooth and sinister image of the vampire nobleman. Christopher Lee was to continue this portrayal.

Browning's *Freaks* (1932), is one of the least seen of all masterpieces of the cinema.

Karloff is crucified by the peasant mob in *The Bride of Frankenstein* (1935).

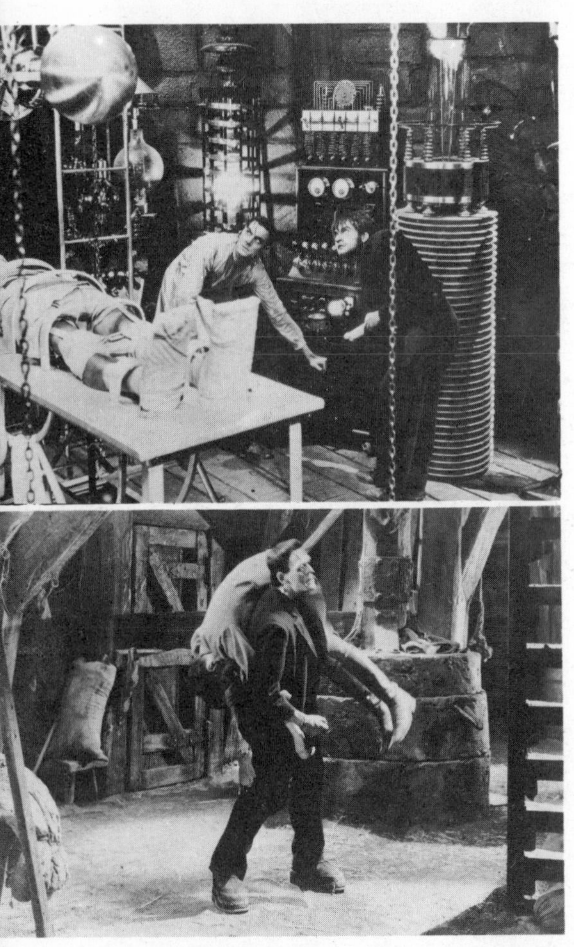

Count Frankenstein creates his suffering monster in James Whale's *Frankenstein* (1931), and a genre is born in the cinema.

James Whale's *Frankenstein* with Boris Karloff, and its successor, *The Bride of Frankenstein*, raised American horror films to a level of high art. Although Karloff's movements also derived from Wegener's Golem, his restrained suffering and extraordinary make-up made him the archetype of man-made monsters on the screen. His cosmetic creator, Jack Pierce, discarded a mythological mask in favour of a pseudo-scientific one, based on "research in anatomy, surgery, criminology, ancient and modern burial customs, and electro-dynamics". The monster was "an electrical gadget". Lightning was "his life force". Although Whale's lighting and symbolism harked back to the myths, particularly when his monster is crucified in the second film, Karloff's playing shows a mechanical being struggling to contain an emotion. He is the embodiment of the robot seeking for a soul in Karel Capek's seminal robot play of 1921, *R.U.R.* The American dream preferred a mechanical horror to a magic one.

Whale made two other fine films between his twin Frankenstein pictures. *The Old Dark House* somewhat failed when the gothic element was stressed, while *The Invisible Man* succeeded when the science fiction of H. G. Wells was again used as a source. In the second film, Claude Rains' non-appearance is the best piece of absent acting in the history of cinema.

Claude Rains is present and absent in *The Invisible Man* (1933).

Yet in this astonishingly fertile period in the history of the American fantasy cinema – perhaps partially a by-product of the mass wish to escape into dreams during the Great Depression – the most successful films of sadism and of monsters were made by the same producer-director team, Merian Cooper and Ernest Schoedsack. In their *The Most Dangerous Game* (made with Irvin Pichel, who also shot a version of *She*) the wicked Count Zaroff lives in a Sadean castle on a mysterious tropical island. There he hunts down shipwrecked sailors with mastiffs and a bow, unless they wish for passive decapitation. The hero Rainsford survives the manhunt and returns in time to save the fair Eve from Zaroff's embrace – "After the hunt, the love!" Throughout the film, torture, terror and eroticism mount to a final climax of death and escape. Cooper and Schoedsack followed with *King Kong*. Using the talent of Edgar Wallace to plot the movie, although he himself borrowed heavily from Conan Doyle's *The Lost World*, the story of the giant ape in his prehistoric domain on Skull Island was created in cooperation with the skills of Willis O'Brien. O'Brien's practical imagination worked out the technicalities by which a puppet could become a gigantic ape and a monstrous furry mask could show bewilderment and anguish as well as rage. The eroticism of King Kong slowly pulling off the shrieking Fay Wray's white satin clothes as carefully as a boy pulls the wings off a gilded fly has haunted a million dreams, while the symbolism of the love-mad ape smashing through New York in search of the girl and finally ending on the pinnacle of the Empire State building swatting fighter-planes like gnats is also archetypal. The savagery and sadness of lust and freedom is set against the cold mechanical death of the city and civilisation. The Kong in each of us dies for a white

The evil Count hunts down the sailor in *The Most Dangerous Game* (1932).

The monster ape rampages to his death on top of the Empire State Building.

sacrificial maiden who leads us to the mechanical crucifixions of the Metropolis.

If *King Kong* and its host of ever-diminishing imitators like *Son of Kong* conjured up the monster movie, *Flash Gordon* in the most famous serial ever made took space travel into the eyes and dreams of the schoolboys of the world. Looking suspiciously like Lang's blond Siegfried, Buster Crabbe as Flash Gordon substitutes a rocket for a white horse and charges off with his sacrificial maiden Dale Arden to do battle with the extra-terrestial forces of evil on the planet Mongo. On a budget as tenuous as the story-line, Flash Gordon battles with mysterious monsters and lion men and humanoids, endlessly saves Dale from the wicked Emperor Ming – a sort of incarnate Yellow Peril – and submerges to underwater cities when not changing planets. The whole serial is one of marvellous ingenuity where cheap versions of most of the monster and mechanical legends are

Flash Gordon (1936–40) is still the doyen of all serials.

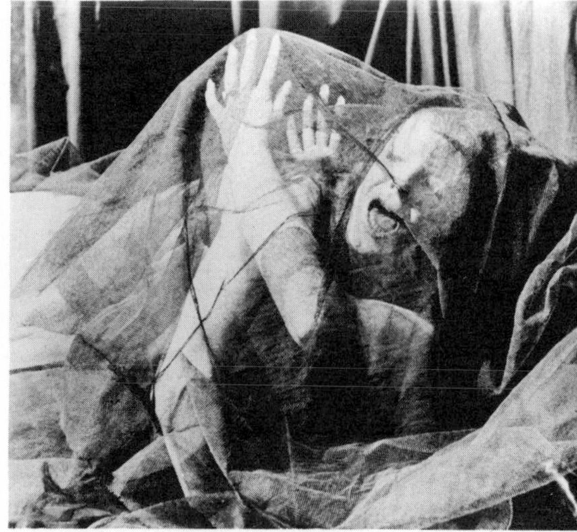

Roger Corman's version of Edgar Allen Poe's *The Tomb of Ligeia* (1964).

set up for the cosmic battles of the wooden and wondrous superhero. The seductive naïveté of the serial merely proves the strength of its archetypes to child or later man. The legend of the hero destroying great beasts and saving maidens on fantastic voyages is common to all ages at all times.

The growth of psychiatry, particularly Jungian, did much to explain the popularity of fantasy films. In his interesting final illustrated work with his pupils, *Man and His Symbols*, Jung and his collaborators regularly use film stills to illustrate the present version of many of the shapes taken from the "collective unconscious." Old symbols do not die, they are reborn in modern form. If the thirteenth-century mystic Ramon Lull in a vision could meet his love with her breast rotten with cancer, we can see in the many versions of *She* or vampire ladies a young woman becoming corrupt before our eyes. If the

Siegfried slays the Dragon in Lang's version of Wagner, but the Dragon itself is as mechanical as any rocket.

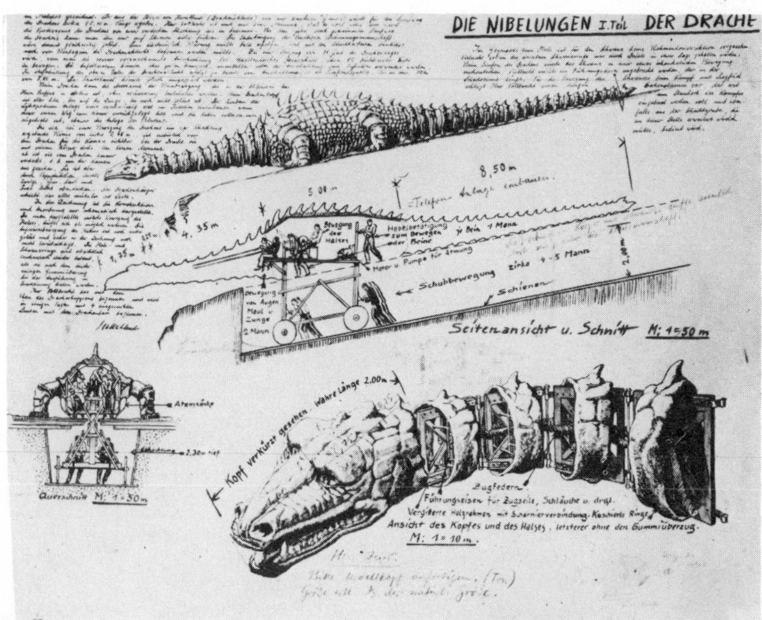

winged snake of Egypt can be the symbol of the rise from the unconscious depths to the sublime, it can also be a medieval dragon slain by a superhero, and end as the winged rocket of an interplanetary explorer rising from a cavern into the unknown. A movie uses old symbols processed by new dream machines.

Yet knowledge of Jung made the naïve symbolism of *Flash Gordon* the conscious symbolism of later space epics such as *2001*. And Freud also was to add a self-awareness to the first fine careless rapture of movie-making, when things just happened and motives were damned. The actual invention of the talking cinema in the late 1920s at the same time as the Great Crash provided an outlet for the ears and frustrations of the unemployed masses – when they could afford the price of a seat in a cinema. And the talkies played into the beliefs of the Freudians, that actions should be explained and motivated. The early process of recording sound was terrible, when two actors were stuck in front of the camera to deliver their dialogue as if set in treacle, because they could not move away from the microphone. But the invention of the travelling boom allowed the actors to move and talk too much. Although the great fantasy movies still kept their words to a minimum and added only the supernatural marvels of sound effects, much of the magic of the silent cinema was sacrificed by explanations of events, which simply could not be crammed into the old title cards. Although Freudianism was little seen in fantasy movies before the 1940s and Val Lewton's minor classics of horror through suggestion, Freud's influence on American producers and screenwriters was to make them verbose. The mystery of every silent film was lost in the urge to motivate every talking film. And in the need to record the onset of the Second World War, the wordy documentary replaced the supernatural movie. What fantasy film could rival the reality of Hitler? What horror film could match the acts of the Nazis?

NIGHTMARES

Lon Chaney Jr. plays the monster role in *The Ghost of Frankenstein* (1942)

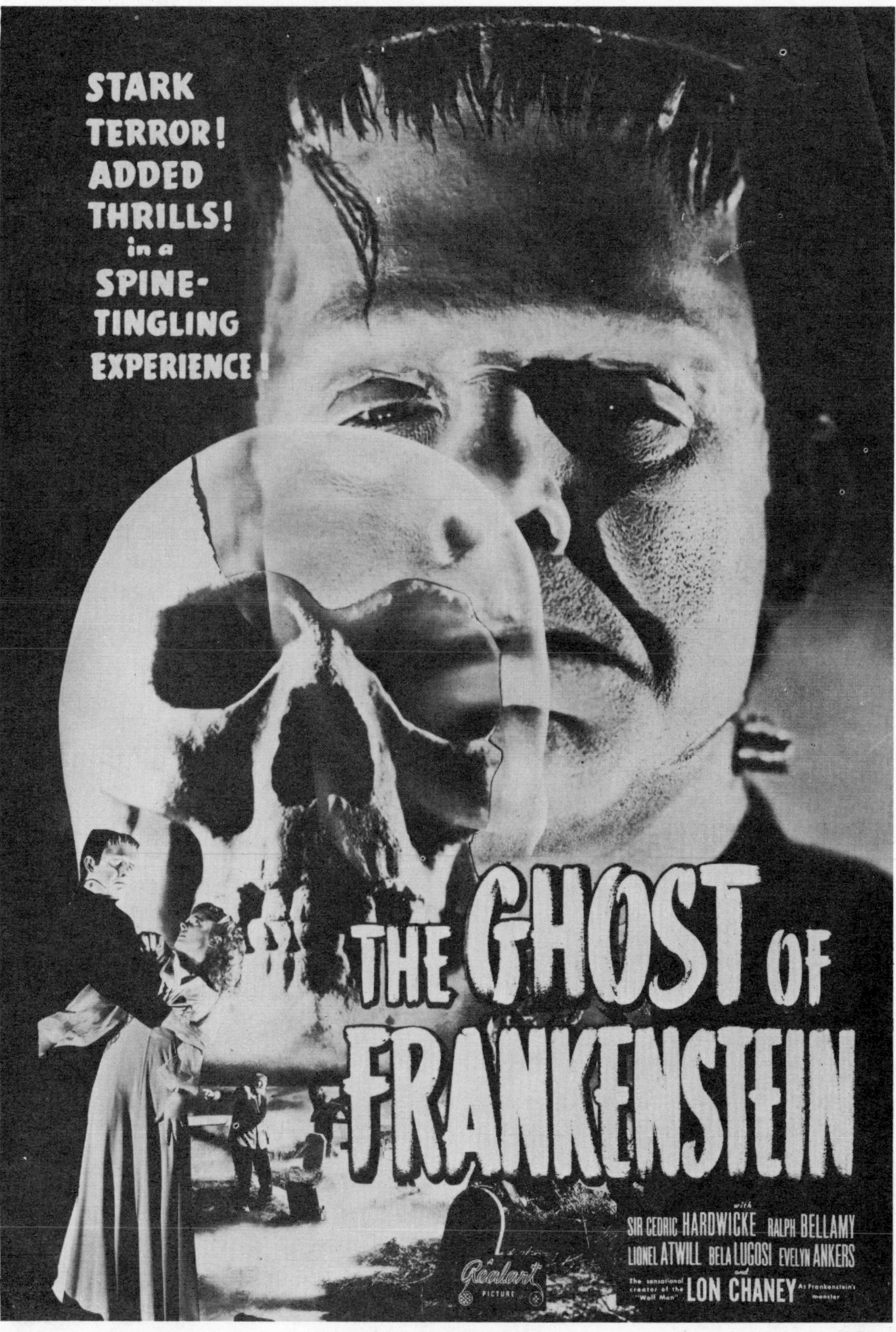

War often has a calming effect on people not directly in the line of fire. They know what they are doing at last. Their lives are given to a national purpose, their cares become the responsibility of the state, their hopes are postponed until after the war. There is no need for the beasts of the subconscious – there is the enemy. The delight in man-made monsters is transferred to the engines of war, admired if friendly, execrated if not. Sufficient thrills are to be found in the daily reports of distant battles. Documentaries provide all the wish-fulfilments of heroism, particularly when made by patriotic propaganda machines, set to manufacturing duty rather than dreams. In time of war, survival is all and dreams relate to peace and men coming home. Fantasy is buried until after the bombardments.

In Nazi Germany, there were no fantasy films, merely romanticised visions of *blitzkrieg* and triumph. In Russia, Stalin's double was always in shot, smiling and leading the resistance like an omnipresent Czar. In Britain too, the great British school of documentary led by Grierson and Jennings came into its own, with Olivier's and Churchill's voices rolling out disembodied over the white cliffs of Dover, and London burning more satisfactorily in the blitz than any model of *Things to Come*. In the United States, insulated at home from both the European and the Pacific War, fantasy films still appeared, losing steadily in popularity and quality. Although Hal Roach's *One Million B.C.*, helped by the aged D. W. Griffith, had something of the spectacular in its dressed-up lizards, and set Lon Chaney Jr. in his father's footsteps, the sequel pictures to earlier successes declined from *Ghost of Frankenstein* to *Son of Dracula* to *The Return of the Vampire* and finally to the rags and tatters of the decaying shroud of a tradition. Only in B pictures with low budgets did the

Simone Simon remembers Balkan black magic in *Cat People* (1942), while Frances Dee walked with a Zombie (1943).

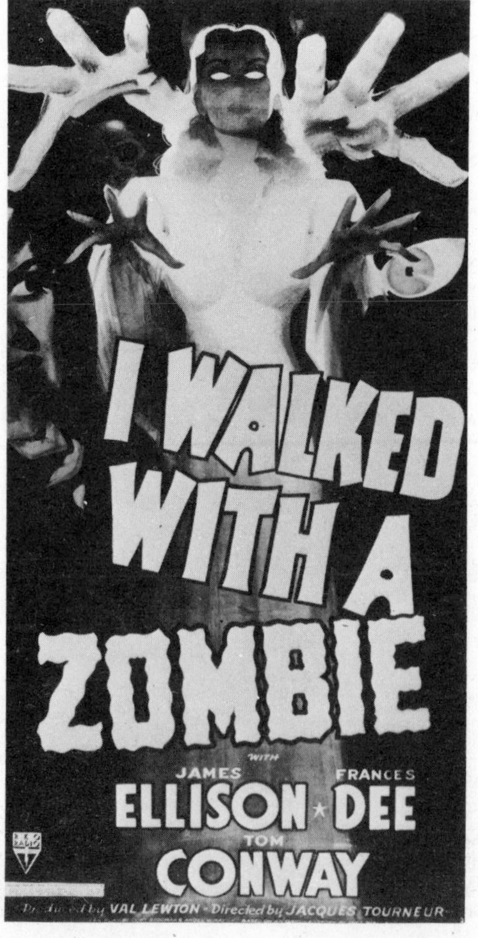

seeds of the fantasy film put out new shoots. There Val Lewton developed the cinema of suggestion, the hinting at horror without showing it, the psychological fear more terrifying than the actual sight of the beast. His *Cat People* and *The Curse of the Cat People* changed the look of horror films. The black leopard was the beast of the unconscious. Internal fear was the external killer. Freud was explicit.

In fact, the fantasies engaged by the World War led to the mockery of the old genres of fantasy. Bela Lugosi now played with the East Side Kids in *Spooks Run Wild* and *Ghosts on the Loose*. The potential idiocy of the genre led to Frankenstein's monster appearing as a gag in *Hellzapoppin'* and W. C. Fields disappearing in free-fall flight onto a lost world to meet a gorilla and a girl who had never been kissed in *Never Give a Sucker an Even Break*. The lunacy of war comedy engaged the audiences from the Marx Brothers' capers to the Crosby and Hope pictures with Dorothy Lamour that were to end in *The Road to Hong Kong* with the twin comics on a womanless planet called Plutonium. Perhaps Abbott and Costello were to take the ridicule of the fantasy film to its furthest limits when they were to meet Frankenstein, Dr. Jekyll and Mr. Hyde, and take a trip to Mars. The irreverence bred by war shook the monsters in their stride. They were never quite so ghastly again. What was a little screen blood to the carnage at Stalingrad? It was no coincidence that Kurt Vonnegut was to take a comic and cosmic way out of his experience of the burning of Dresden. When *Slaughterhouse Five* was finally written and filmed, the cinders of war ended in a celestial penthouse. The horror of battle finished as a space joke.

W. C. Fields meets the gorilla in *Never Give a Sucker an Even Break* (1941).

In *Les Enfants du paradis* (1944), the nostalgia for a past that was better than now is caught by Barrault and Arletty.

Arletty in *Les Visiteurs du soir* (1942), lives in an enchanted medieval world . . .

In occupied France, however, the film-makers chose the way that the German cinema had chosen after the defeat of the First World War. Forbidden by the Nazis and the Vichy government to take any political stance that might suggest independence, the French directors hid in fantasy and in the past from the daily compromises of their collaboration with the Germans. Carné produced two masterpieces, *Les Enfants du paradis* and *Les Visiteurs du soir*. They were a far cry from the realism of his *Le Jour se lève*. In *Les Enfants du paradis*, set in Paris in 1840, Jean-Louis Barrault in his white clown-suit creates a masterpiece of mime, and even when Arletty teaches him a little of the realities of love, he cannot escape from his sentimental world of clowns and fancies. Even more unreal and metaphysical is *Les Visiteurs du soir*, in which Arletty appears dressed as a youth and a medieval legend unfolds in love and tears and magic. It reeks of a nostalgia for a time that never was, an escape through the heart from the horror of defeat and collaboration. The final working out of this vein of escapism is shown in Cocteau's *La Belle et la bête*, which was shot in 1945. There the story of the redemption of the beast by the love of a young maiden satisfies an archetypal myth. It is also an unconscious plea for mercy for those who may have seemed horrible by acquiescing in the Vichy regime, but who really loved France in their hearts. As with Jean Marais, the foul visage of war can drop off and show the fair face of peace. Cocteau's extraordinary prewar beginning as a surrealist director in *Le Sang d'un poète*, where he uses printed negative to show a dreamlike journey down a hotel corridor, achieves its apogee in this mythical apologia for defeated France asking to be redeemed by love, not by the vengeance of the Free French.

. . . and is turned into stone for her love's sake.

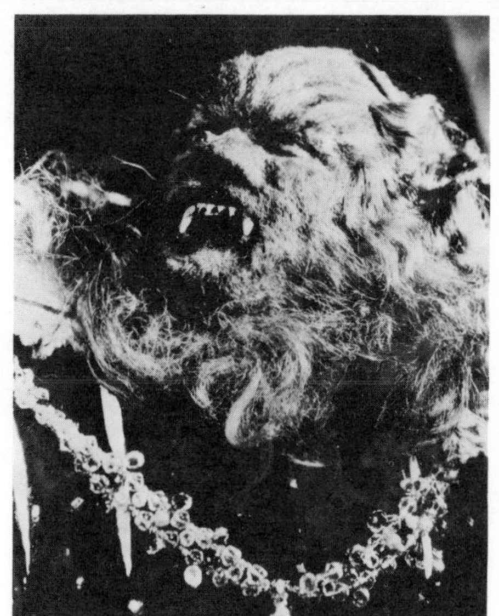

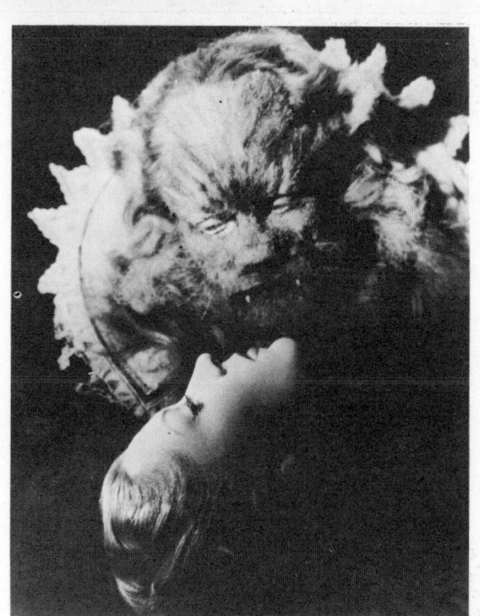

Jean Marais as the Beast in Cocteau's *La Belle et la bête* (1946).

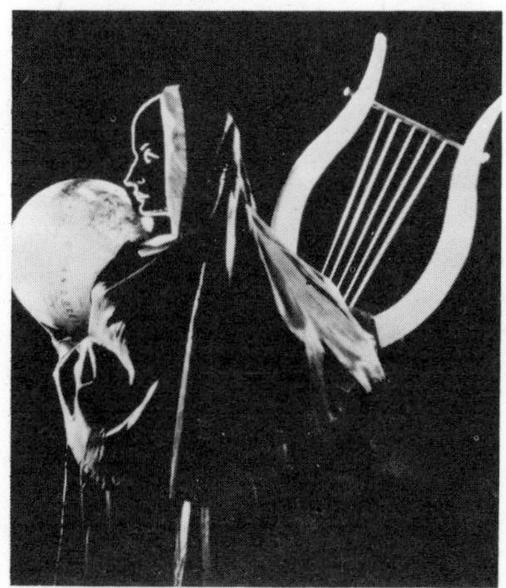

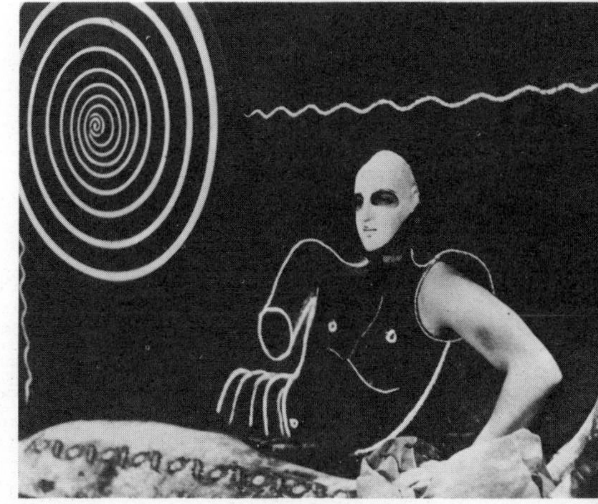

Cocteau printed negative film and used other novel techniques to suggest a dream journey in his *Le Sang d'un poète* (1930).

In Italy, however, defeat at the end of the war led to the opposite reaction, films of bitter realism. The actuality of *Rome Open City* and *Bicycle Thieves* made even the British documentaries look stagey. With Mussolini, fantasy also died in the Italian cinema until the later age of Fellini. Yet in Japan, which also was to begin its great period of film-making with its defeat, Kurosawa's *Rashomon* and *Seven Samurai* and *Throne of Blood* brought a new dramatic, historic and exaggerated cinema to the West. The ambiguities of *Rashomon* and the battles of the armoured Samurai as fierce and scaly as small dragons created a Japanese idiom both subtle and nostalgic, dangerous and mythic that engaged the national mind in the fantasies of better times gone by. Although Kurosawa himself was to work in the realist cinema, as in his classic *Ikiru* (still the best film made about the horrors of urban government), the Japanese cinema has remained most successfully international

Kurosawa's *Rashomon* (1950) and *Seven Samurai* (1954), taught the western cinema that Japan had learned its lessons and was producing a great national cinema of its own.

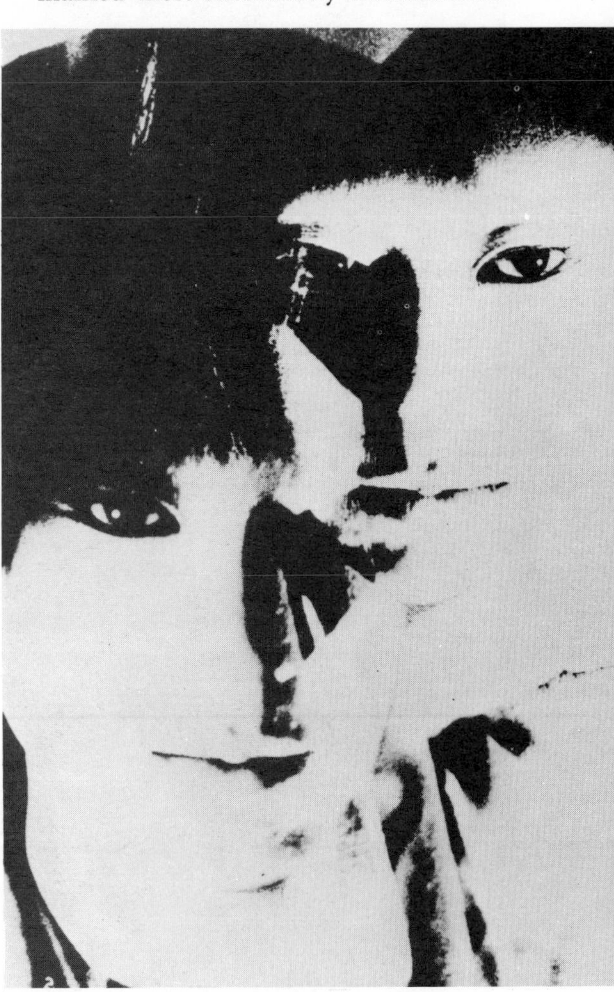

The faces of ghosts from *Kwaidan* (1964).

when it has devoted itself to Samurai stories or ghost stories, such as the three tales of the fantastic *Kwaidan*. The Toho imitations of the monster genre – often based on Godzilla, who in turn is based on Gwangi – are also successful, although they are cheapened versions of extraordinary originals. When Godzilla meets King Kong, for instance, it looks like a big lizard playing with a man in a monkey suit and destroying scaled-down models of cities. The Toho special effects man, Tsuburuya, was no match for O'Brien or Harryhausen. In fact, the latest world-wide craze for Kung-Fu films, where the super hero chops and leaps his or her way to victory over thirty villains at a time is far more acrobatic and fantastic than the mediocre monster offerings. Inevitably, the British horror specialists, Hammer Films, have made a Kung-Fu gothic creation in Hong Kong, called *The Legend of the Seven Golden Vampires*. The vampire meets the karate chop, Dracula meets a Fairbanks Fu Manchu, the fang is not mightier than the fist.

A Japanese temple is pulled down by the two playful monsters in *King Kong versus Godzilla* (1963).

In Britain, indeed, Hammer Films revived and renewed the gothic tradition that dated from Frankenstein and Dracula. New stars were discovered to replace Lugosi and Karloff, notably Christopher Lee and Peter Cushing. Emphasising blood to suit post-war colour film and tastes, *The Curse of Frankenstein* began a cycle of remakes that involved more and more sex until Ingrid Pitt was biting the breasts of her victims in *The Vampire Lovers*. Parallel with its gothic offerings, Hammer made *The Quatermass Xperiment*, which had both space rockets and a monster electrocuted in Westminster Abbey. But its biggest venture into space, *Moon Zero Two*, was outshot by the real landings on the moon. Jules Verne and H. G. Wells had become documentaries. The old African fantasies, *She* and *The Return of She*, and dreams of prehistory, *One Million Years B.C.* and *Creatures the World Forgot*, proved more successful for Hammer than exploring the Universe. The ancient myths were more profitable than the modern facts.

Slow decomposition in *The Quatermass Xperiment* (1955).

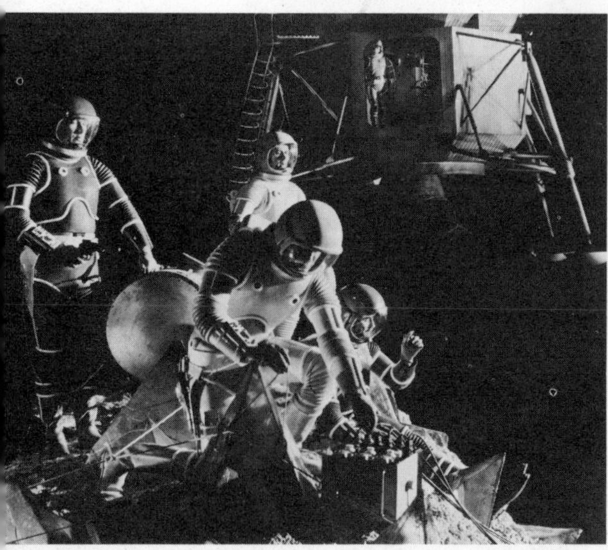

The astronauts land on the moon in *Moon Zero Two* (1969).

Human sacrifice in *Creatures the World Forgot* (1971).

In the United States, Roger Corman, working for American International Pictures, used Edgar Allen Poe's eerie stories as the basis for his shoot-and-run movies that always kept their tongues in their cheeks and their eyes on the budgets. Peter Lorre played in his last guest role for Corman in *The Raven* and Vincent Price took over from Karloff as the prince of demons. His work in the *House of Usher* and *The Masque of the Red Death* and *The Tomb of Ligeia* gave a new emphasis to horror films, a decadent menace, an amused shiver, a weary thrill. Whatever he did with Corman had an elegance which hid the fact that the costs of making the picture were cut more to the bone than any screen victim.

Peter Lorre and Vincent Price as birds of prey in *The Raven* (1963)

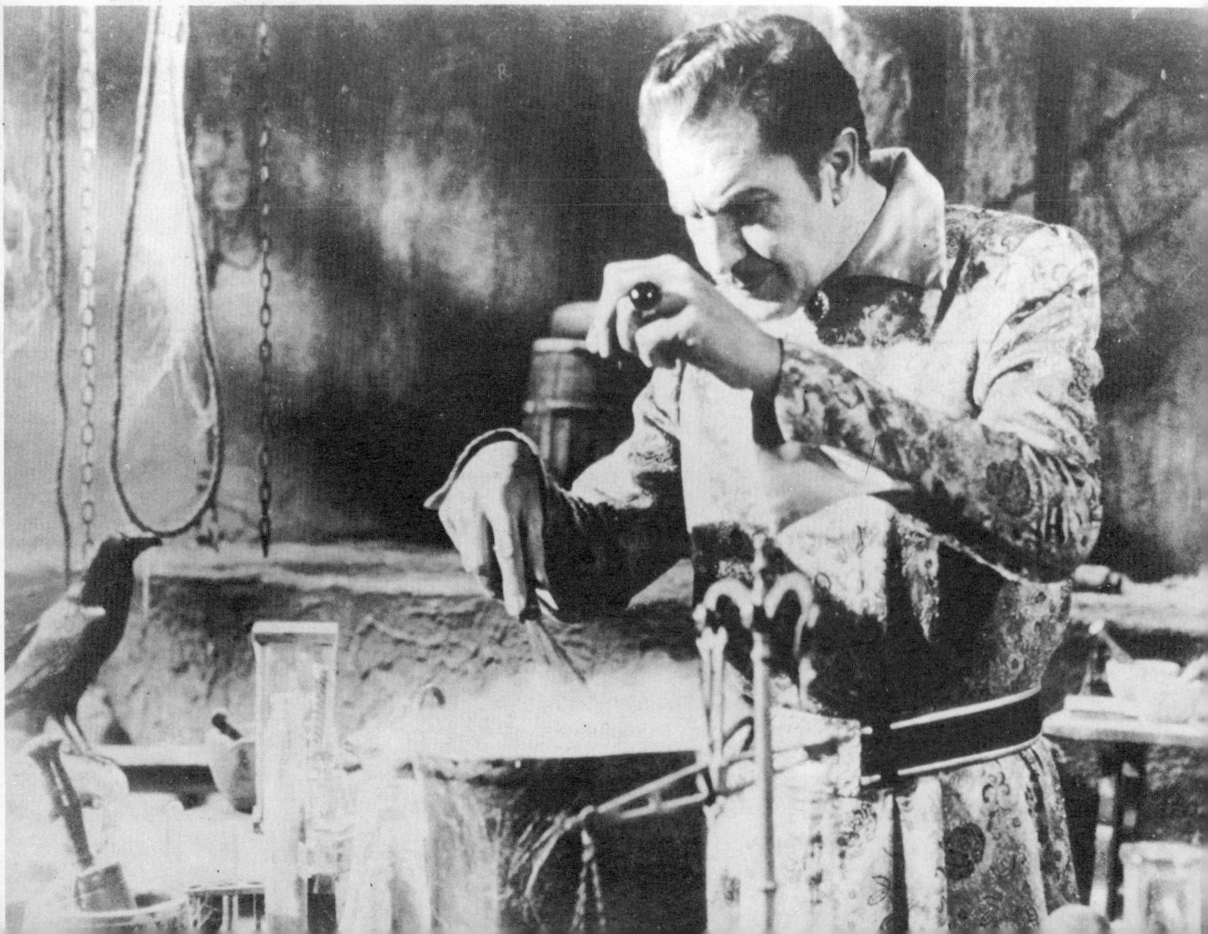

The House of Usher (1960) takes some time to fall in Corman's version of Poe.

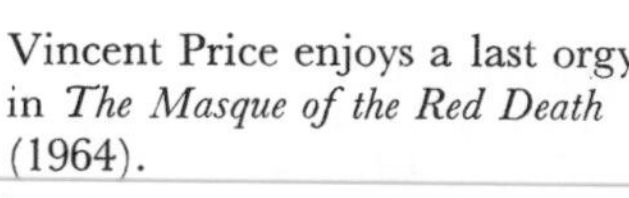

Vincent Price enjoys a last orgy in *The Masque of the Red Death* (1964).

Ligeia will not die in Corman's *The Tomb of Ligeia* (1964).

Barbara Steele, the favourite Italian vampire lady, in *The Revenge of the Vampire* (1960).

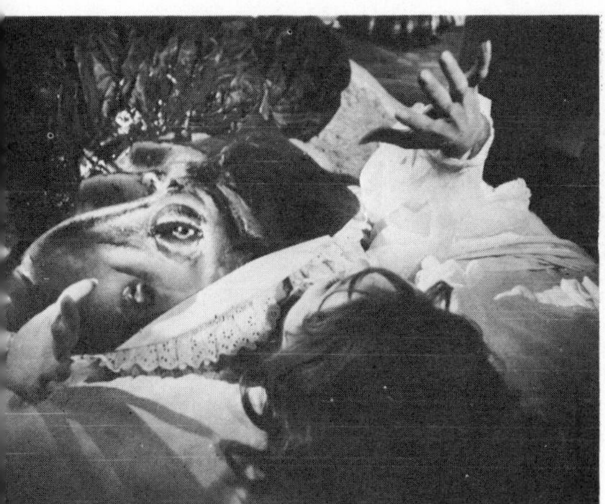

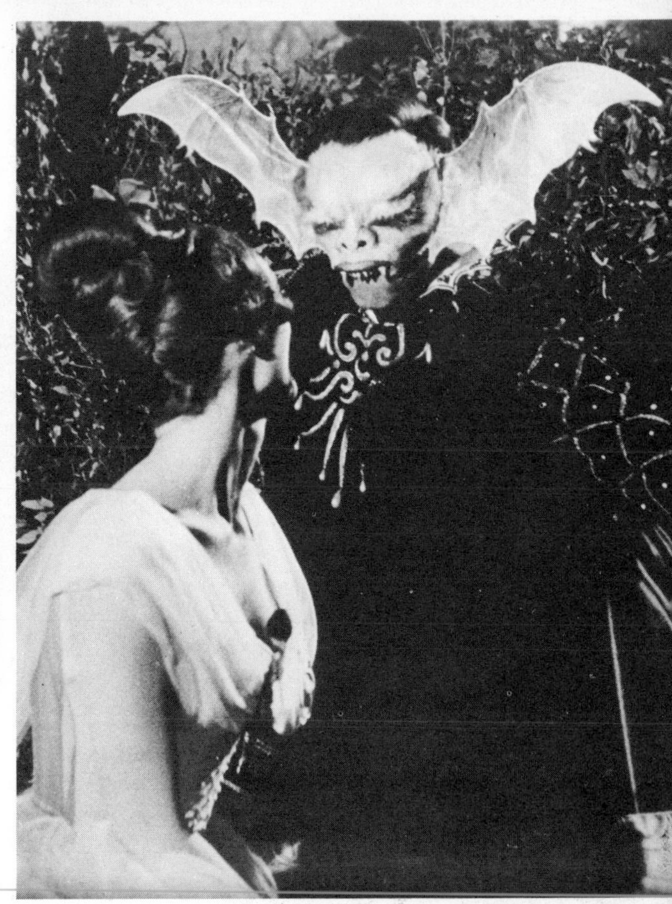

Roger Vadim's *Blood and Roses* (1960).

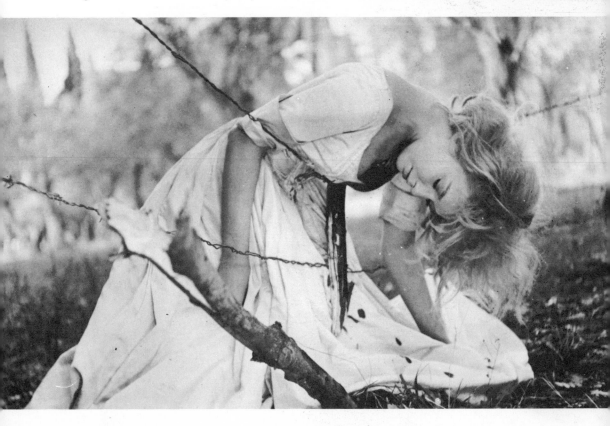

Only Mario Bava's vampire pictures in Italy equalled the lush frenzies of Hammer and American International. Other imitations of the genre in Spain and France merely exploited the sexual fantasies, implicit in the material and now exaggerated to the point of ridicule. Roger Vadim, who nearly succeeded later with erotic fantasies of the cosmic space-strip *Barbarella*, failed badly with his lesbian vampire picture, *Blood and Roses*.

The latest vampire pictures from France can go little further in visibility. Where every horror was suggested by Val Lewton, every variation on Krafft-Ebbing and Sacher-Masoch and Montague Summers is now shown luridly and cut-price. The work of Jean Rollin is the full-frontal end to the vampire's rise from the grave. The superb Jack Palance was even persuaded into making a version of de Sade's *Justine*, which did not help his reputation.

Barbarella (1968) owes all to the beauty of Jane Fonda and little to a space trip.

Images from the sex vampire films of Jean Rollin (and on two following pages).

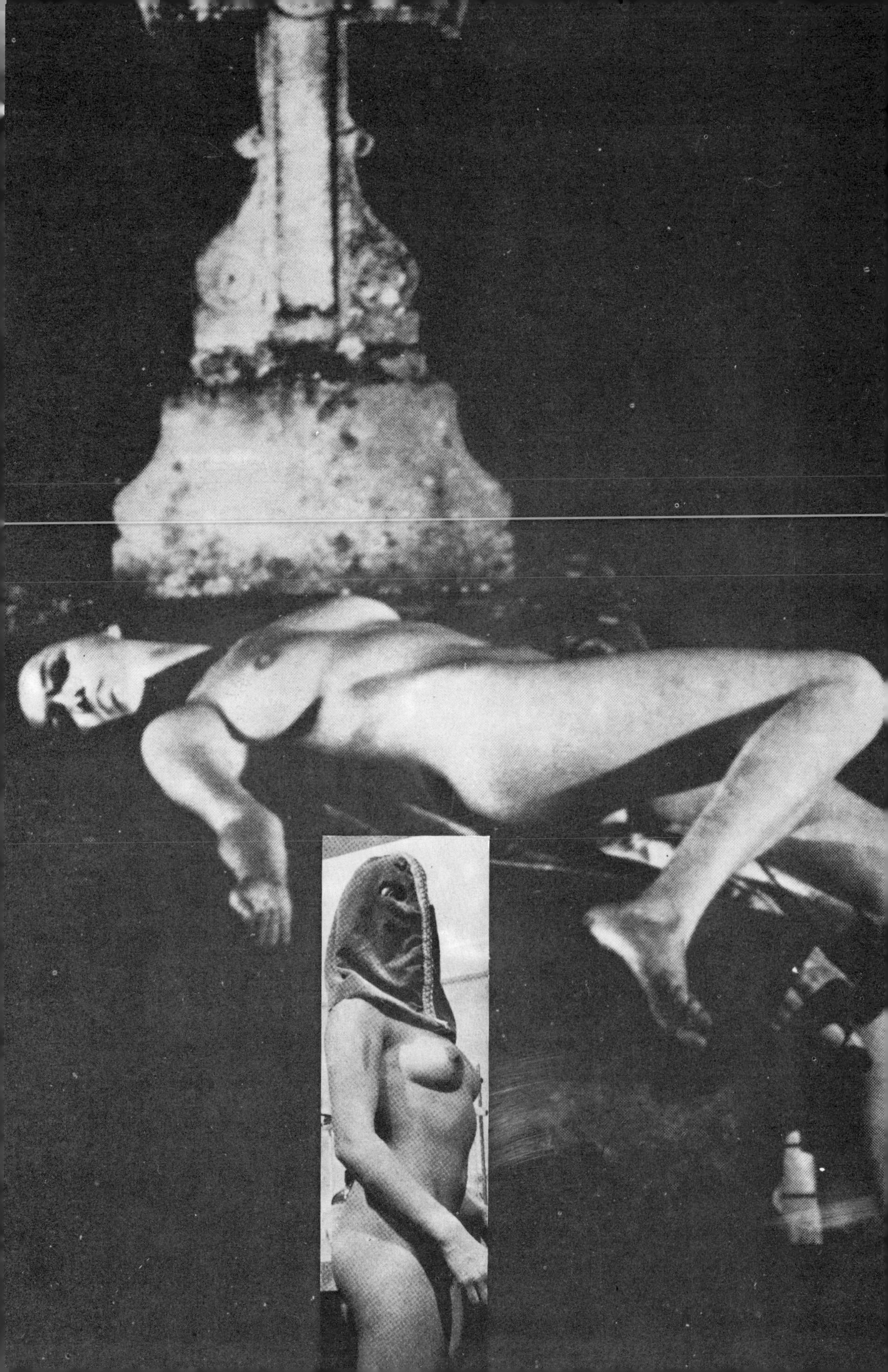

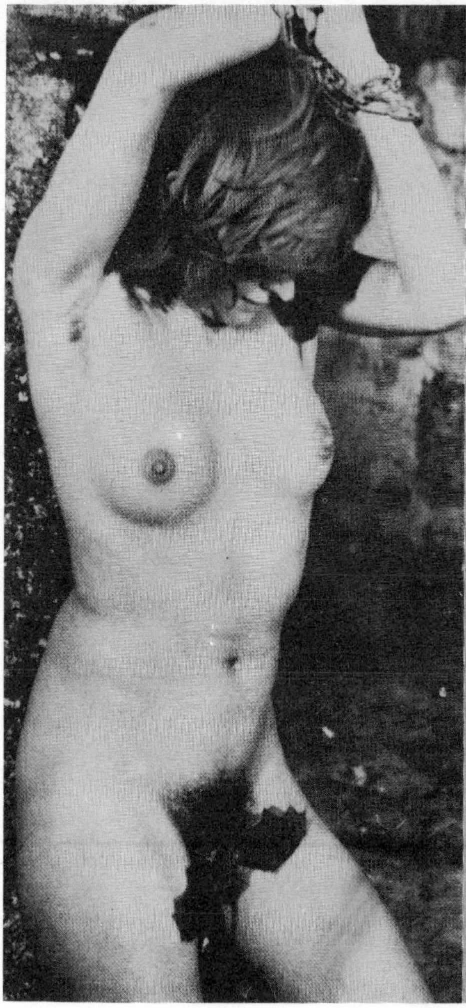

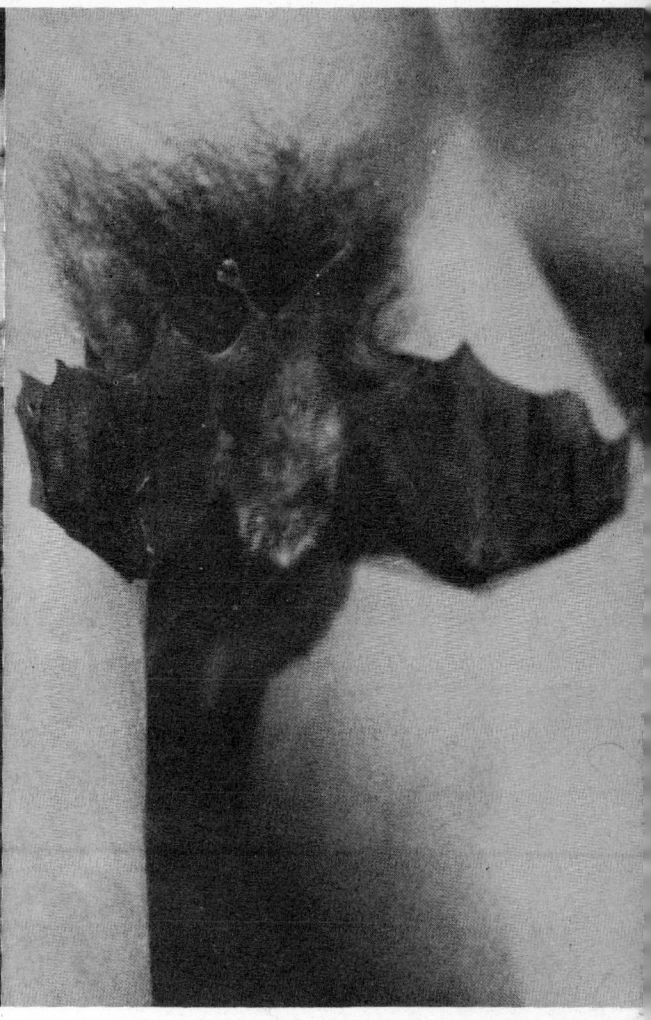

Jack Palance considers his victim in *Justine* (1969), directed by Jesus Franco.

Catherine Deneuve lives out her sexual fantasies in *Belle de Jour* (1967).

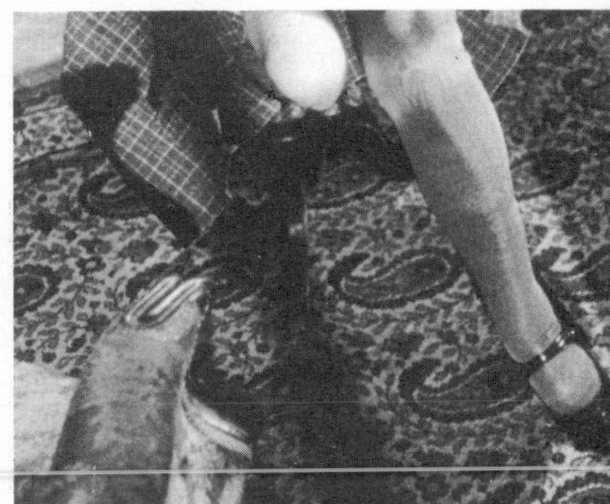

Again Deneuve, this time with a false leg, has visions in *Tristana* (1970).

The French schoolboys riot in Jean Vigo's *Zéro de conduite* (1933).

Yet if some traditions of the fantasy cinema were being vulgarised to perdition, others were safe in the hands of the old and the young masters. Luis Bunuel still used fantasy and horror with great discretion – the mysterious buzzing box and the dreams of torture of *Belle de Jour* and the bell-clapper with a human head and the amputated leg of *Tristana*. In England, Lindsay Anderson carried on the tradition of Jean Vigo's *Zéro de conduite*. This famous anarchistic attack on the system of boy's schools involved surrealist techniques – a dwarf headmaster, a slow-motion pillow-fight, a bombardment of the prizegiving by the boys from the school roof. Anderson's *If* used similar fantasy sequences to expose the oppressions of the English public-school system. Both films express masterfully the dreams of outrage and rebellion that torment the inward souls of schoolboys locked in with their books and masters to learn what they cannot use. Also Arrabal's theatre work had its influence on the cinema, especially in the underrated *Le Grand cérémonial*.

Similar schoolboy revolutionary fantasies occur in Lindsay Anderson's *If . . .* (1968).

Dolls at play in *Le Grand cérémonial* (1970).

In the United States, however, the dropping of the atomic bombs on Japan and the horrific consequences of radiation spawned variations on the old fantasy themes of mutation and transplants and monsters and space travel and total destruction. Howard Hawks transposed the values of the Western and the heroic war film to extraterrestrial dimensions. In *The Thing* of 1951, a small group of American military men are set in the Arctic against a humanoid monster from outer space which has arrived in an auto-destructive flying saucer. The Thing has an arm which the dogs chew off "just like a super carrot", but it lives on blood which it drains off living things. It is set alight with kerosene and finally electrocuted to cinders, with a Dr. Carrington playing the original Count Frankenstein role and protesting, "I'm not your enemy, I'm a scientist", and getting struck down by The Thing for his pains. The film ends in an epilogue warning "*Watch the skies!*" The ancient winged god of death, the Grendel of Beowulf, the annihilation of the atom bomb: these are preludes to the final end of

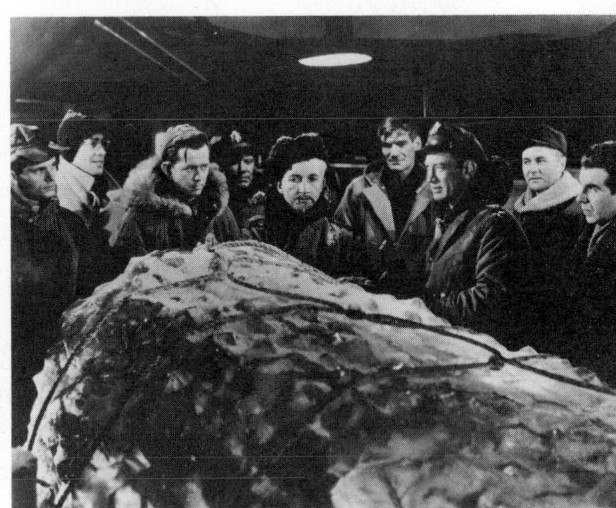

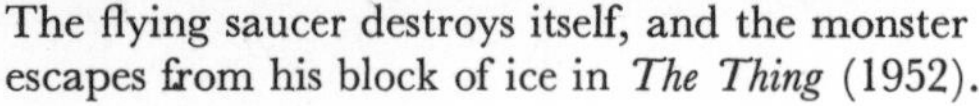

The flying saucer destroys itself, and the monster escapes from his block of ice in *The Thing* (1952).

The model city burns in *Gog* (1954).

the world from an angry heaven by God or monster or Unidentified Flying Object. "*Watch the skies!*"

The success and intelligence of *The Thing* bred a host of lesser imitators. George Pal went back to H. G. Wells for *The War of the Worlds*, but he updated the setting of the Martian invasion from Victorian Woking to modern Los Angeles. Yet the world was not saved from the invaders from Mars by the atom bomb, but by the common cold – a victory for democratic values. *Gog*, a monster originally from British mythology and the Book of Revelations, turns out to be a rebel robot and the cities that are destroyed at Armageddon suggest models more than mayhem. In *Donovan's Brain*, intelligence and willpower are reduced literally to a resurrected brain – why need a body to dominate men when the mind is all? But among these pale and anaemic venturings into the new world suggested by the brilliant post-war science-fiction writers, only four films of the 1950s after *The Thing* achieved a certain kind of lasting reputation in the United States.

The earth is under attack in *The War of the Worlds* (1953).

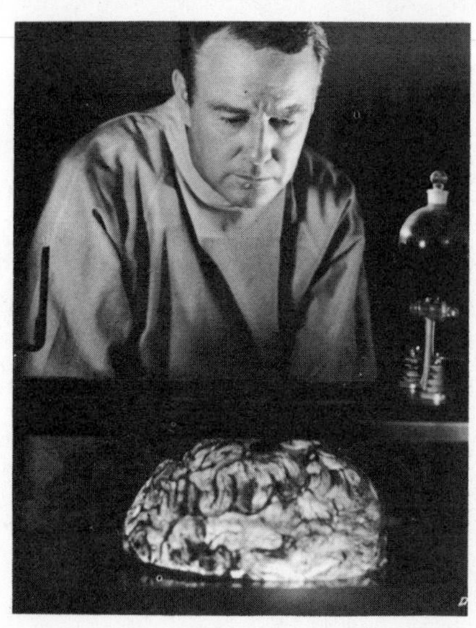

Lew Ayres as the scientist who becomes the slave to the brain of a dead millionaire in Siodmack's version of *Donovan's Brain* (1953).

The first of these was *The Incredible Shrinking Man*. In it, the hero passes through a strange cloud of radiation and immediately begins to diminish. He is reduced to living in a doll's house and is hunted by his own cat. Finally he wins a battle with a spider, now dwarfing him, and climbs out of a cellar to live in the jungle that is his garden with a message spreading outwards to the stars, that man's spirit is mightier than his size. Another low-budget minor classic was Don Siegel's *Invasion of the Body Snatchers*. In it, replicas of people form inside gigantic seedpods, which then replace the actual humans. This fantasy of brainwashing and transplantation, in which men themselves are taken over by aliens, suited an American audience terrified of subtle indoctrination by communism or fluoride or conspiracy. The original end of the film, where the hero runs against lanes of traffic, warning them uselessly, "*You're next! You're next!*" is a chilling alarm for heedless democracy.

The terrors of being small in *The Incredible Shrinking Man* (1957).

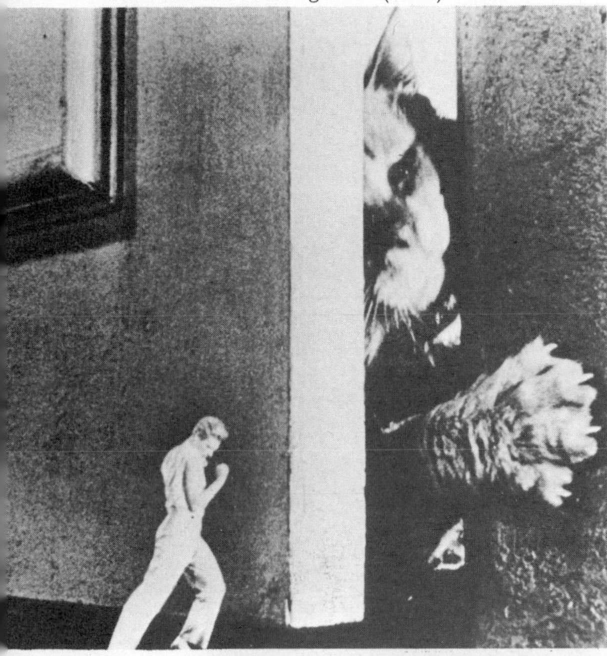

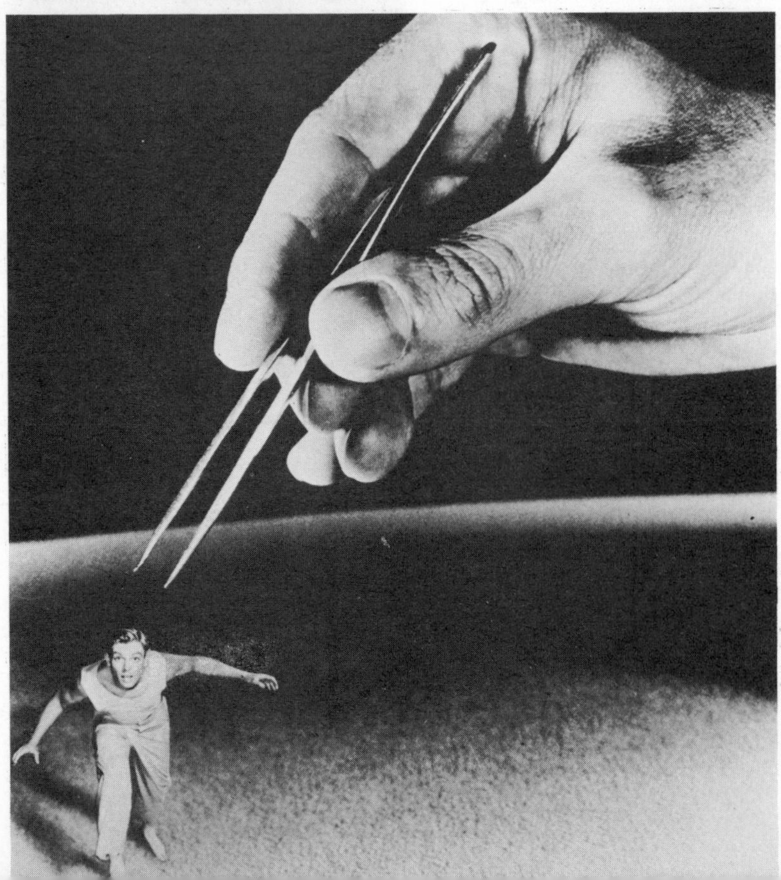

The seed-pod people take over in Siegel's *Invasion of the Body Snatchers* (1956).

In *Forbidden Planet*, however, Freudianism actually produces its first visible monster, the Id. Based on Shakespeare's *The Tempest* with the island now a planet where a spaceship lands and with Prospero himself called Dr. Morbius, the film defines Caliban as the Id – the horrible subconscious of Morbius himself. The good race of this Utopian planet, the Krel, have all dematerialised and escaped into the expanding universe, leaving behind only the demonic monsters of the Id, "the elementary basis of the subconscious mind . . . the mindless beauty of their innermost souls." At last, the gigantic man-destroying Id attacks the Doctor's house and Morbius hears the truth – "That thing out there is *you*!" He screams out, "My evil self is at that door and I have no power to stop it!" But just as all is about to be destroyed, Morbius yells, "I deny you! I give you up!" and he dies. The Id disintegrates, the spaceship escapes. At last, the monster of the subconscious is visualised, and the dragons of old are shown to be dredged from the depths of each man's mind.

Dr. Morbius destroys himself in *Forbidden Planet* (1956) (and on facing page).

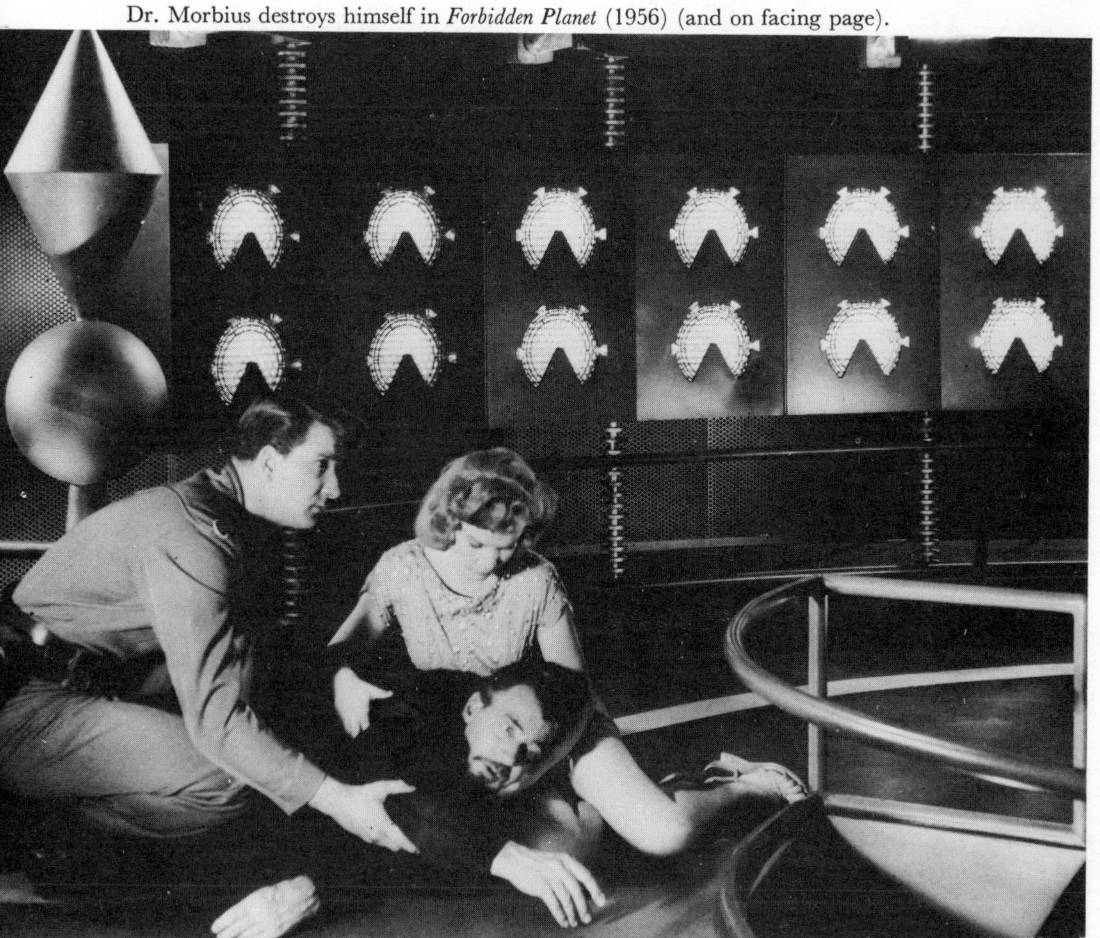

The other Freudian minor classic came from Stanley Kramer. It was based on a script by Dr. Seuss and Allan Scott, *The 5,000 Fingers of Dr. T*. Unjustly neglected except in France, this film is indeed what Columbia billed it, "The Wonder Musical of the Future". Kramer used music as an orchestra of the subconscious to penetrate deep into the caverns of fear and memory. It is a film as frightening and amusing as parts of Disney's *Pinocchio* or *Fantasia*. It is Kramer's genius to equal the animated terrors of the boy-donkeys or the whale through his actors and studio sets. *The 5,000 Fingers of Dr. T* is the best fantasy musical yet made, just as *The Tales of Hoffman* brought the chilling fairy stories of childhood best to the screen in the form of a ballet.

Posters from Stanley Kramer's fantasy musical *The 5,000 Fingers of Dr. T* (1953).

The mechanical doll gets out of control, and the girl-flowers fight among themselves in *The Tales of Hoffman* (1951).

Bookburning in Truffaut's *Fahrenheit 451* (1966).

Whenever a great director worked on a science-fiction theme, something of merit emerged. In France, Jean-Luc Godard's *Alphaville* suggests an amoral urban world of the future; it is a miracle of economic film-making and a prophecy of brain-control. Truffaut's *Farenheit 451* taken from Ray Bradbury's novel is less successful, although more expensive. Its visions of book-burning, however, frighteningly recall the realities of totalitarian thinking from Savanarola to Hitler. Yet perhaps the greatest time-travel film of the 1960s was Chris Marker's *La Jetée* In it, the hero voyages into the future through a grid of lines that make up a picture. Marker's hero also travels through the years in a Proustian rather a Wellsian sense – it is his remembrance of things past in childhood that gives him his time - warp rather than his time machine.

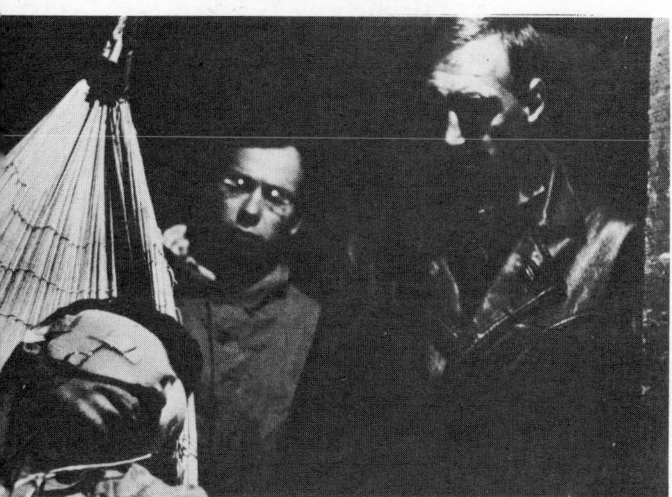

In *La Jetée* (1963), Chris Marker's hero takes a time trip.

The control room in *Dr. Strangelove* (1963), where plans to deliver the terminal bomb, already in the bomb bay, are made.

Yet the greatest fantasy film-maker of them all, Stanley Kubrick, was yet to be known. Brought up from childhood in the atmosphere of old fantasy films, he extended the possibilities of screen imagination in three powerful works, *Dr. Strangelove* and *2001* and *A Clockwork Orange*. *Dr. Strangelove* turned the final destruction of the earth by an atomic explosion into a farce; the ultimate pilot is actually dropped with the terminal bomb. *2001* combined within itself most of dominant themes of fantasy movies – the beginnings of prehistory when man was a lethal ape, futurist space-travel to a space station, the body of an astronaut crumbling to dust, the rebellious robot brain cleverer than his makers, and the final magical trip through space and time and the universe. Kubrick's technique was greater than anything seen before and was only to be approached by the Russian *Solaris*, which also dealt with space stations and memory and time.

2001, made in 1968, is the greatest space epic since *Things to Come*. Again it was made in a British studio. (And on facing page.)

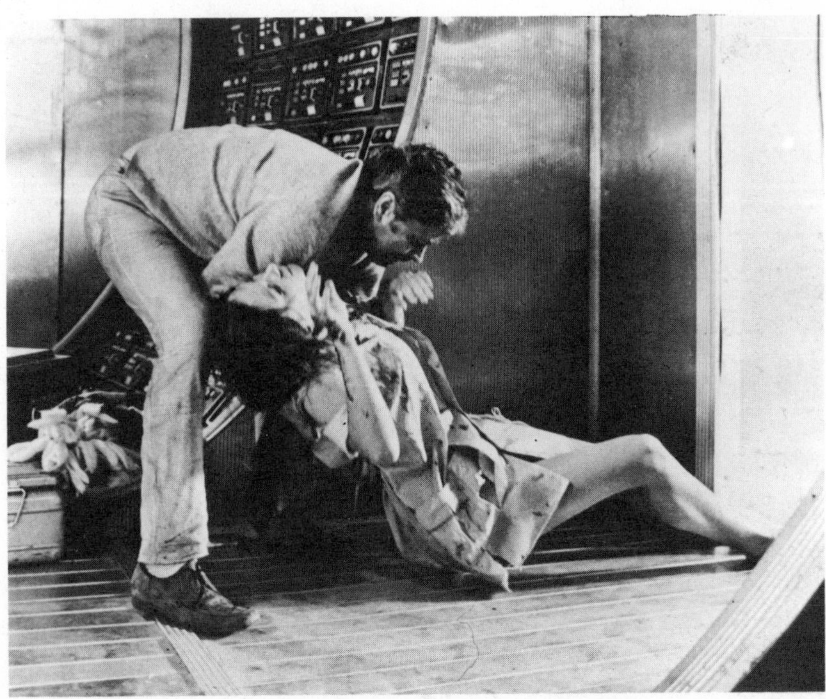

In *Solaris* (1971–72), the Russian astronauts take a trip in time.

A Clockwork Orange, however, showed a world of casual violence and plastic slum that shocked far more than the drab moralities of Orwell's *1984* or the hedonistic hierarchies of Huxley's *Brave New World*. Kubrick's recognisable urban slum with its gangs of sadistic clowns and its coffee-bars based on the erotic fantasies of Allan Jones and its electro-shock therapy in the service of morality was too near the possibility of a horrific future to sit easy on the stomachs of its audience. There is little question that Kubrick has pushed the unsettling powers of the cinema beyond the limits probed by Bunuel. For savagery of image dredged from the depths of the subconscious, Kubrick is the prince of darkness and the apostle of light.

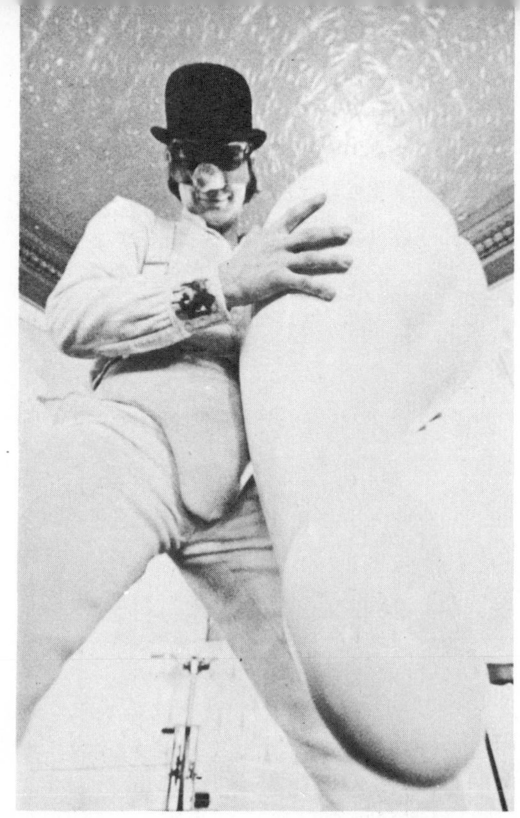

A Clockwork Orange (1971) brought the ultra fantasy of ultra violence too close for comfort.

Fears of final destruction . . .

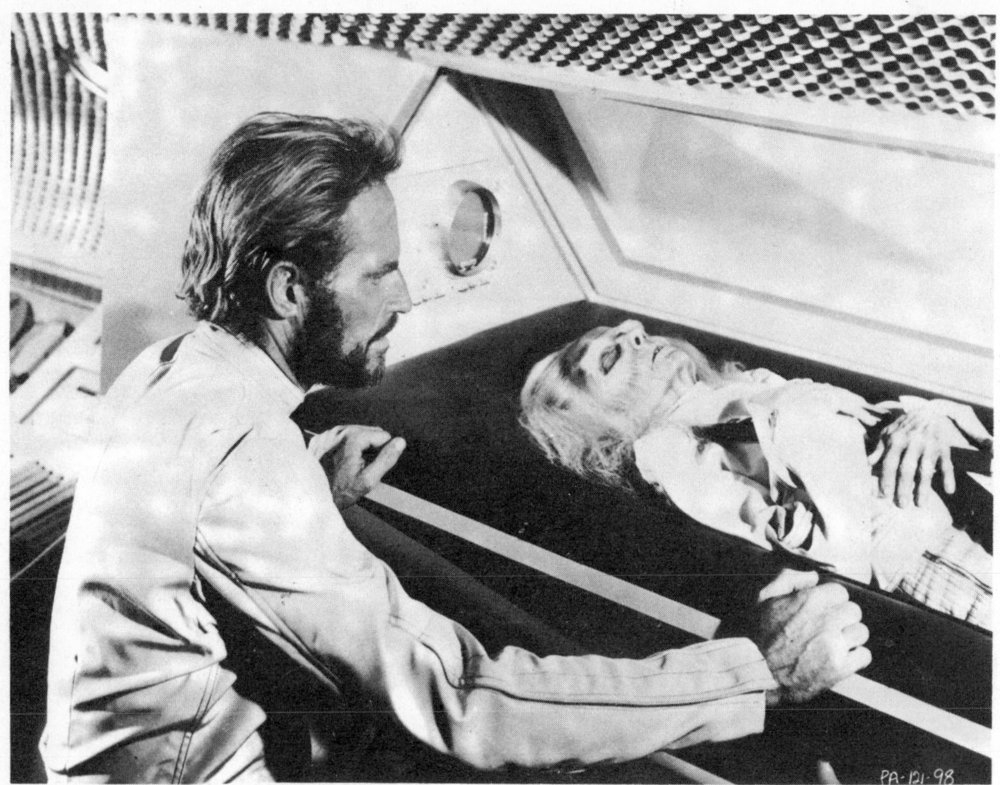

. . . and of our simian origins in *Planet of the Apes* (1967).

So the dream machine has ingested the myths and the mechanical monsters of men's faiths and obsessions, and it has displayed them over the past seventy-five years. At first, the images of the cinema were largely unconscious in their picturing of the unknown, but now they depend on the discoveries of psychiatry as well as of lost continents and planets. From Gilgamesh to Flash Gordon, from Talos to Hal the Computer in *2001*, from Babylon to Hollywood is no great step. The more societies change, the more their images remain the same. Fantasies are constant. The cinema has taken the monsters that psychiatry returned inside us and has put them on show like the paintings on the cavemen's wall. In the illusions of the cinema, we can see our longings and terrors on the loose and at large. In *The Planet of the Apes*, we can enjoy our fears of final destruction and of our monkey origins. In *La Grande Bouffe*, we can outdo a Roman orgy and not vomit. The cine-fantastic is the great synthesiser and the great leveller. It throws open to all the discoveries of the wise and the luxuries of the rich. Before the dream machine, men feared the myths told to them by their priests and kings and powers. With the dream machine, men need no longer fear the fantasies that unroll in front of them at their choice and pleasure. Beyond the dream machine lies the final dream, where every man shall have his fancy evermore and never return to earth again.

Title Index